First published in 1996 by BOTSOTSO PUBLISHING
PO BOX 23910, Joubert Park 2044, Johannesburg, South Africa

ISBN 0-620-20282-3

Copyright in the text © THE BOTSOTSO JESTERS, 1996
Copyright in the illustrations © Anna Varney, 1996

Text: THE BOTSOTSO JESTERS
Illustrations: Anna Varney
Translations: Unless otherwise stipulated are by the poets themselves
Editor: Anna Varney

Layout and design: Michéle Dean
Printed by: House of Print, Johannesburg

Funded by:

STIGTING VIR DIE SKEPPENDE KUNSTE
FOUNDATION FOR THE CREATIVE ARTS

Some of the poems in this book have previously been published in the following publications: Atio, Bliksem, Botsotso, Die Hard Press, Herstoria, Inprint, Like a House on Fire (Cosaw), New Coin, Something Quarterly, Staffrider and Tribute.

CONTENTS

INTRODUCTION 1

PART 1
BOTSOTSO JESTERS 5

PART 2
DUETS 20

PART 3
SIPHIWE KA NGWENYA 25

PART 4
ISABELLA MOTADINYANE 37

PART 5
ALLAN KOLSKI HORWITZ 50

PART 6
IKE MBONENI MUILA 64

PART 7
ANNA VARNEY 79

INTRODUCTION

SIPHIWE KA NGWENYA:
POETRY TALK

When I was in primary school I remember a Parent's Day when I said proudly, " . . . when I grow up I wish to be a lawyer!" But it never worked out. In 1981 a voice came to me in the form of oral poetry. I didn't write in those days, poems came to me in my sleep and during special occasions like parties, weddings and funerals. In 1983 I started writing them down with the intention of reaching a wider audience.

In the late '80's I joined AWA where I met writers like Don "Zinga Special" Mattera and Sipho Sepamla. I used to attend poetry workshops at Funda Centre where at times the security police paid us a visit. Then I switched to COSAW which is where my work developed. At that time my parents, especially my father, used to warn me. To him it was 'only politics'. I used to sneak out from home to go and perform at Regina Mundi. I also teamed up with young poets like Ben Thabo Molefe and Willie Tshaka, until I joined the Botsotso Jesters. What I enjoy is collectivity and experimentation, also our freedom in the use of languages. I also enjoy 'poetry talk' with young poets like Lesego Rampolokeng and Pedi Tlhobolo who are not afraid to express their feelings - but do so in a poetic way, as do Peter Setuke and Ingoapele Madingoane. Now I would love to concentrate on traditional oral/praise/performance poetry because many poets are afraid to trudge on it for fear of being labelled 'backward'. At the same time, I would like to extend these traditional forms and make them more critical and contemparary.

ISABELLA MOTADINYANE:
HOW I FOUND MY POETRY

In 1980 - 1986 I was training in ballet dancing and in 1991, in piano. Well, before that I was doing athletics. But all these activities did not work for me because they did not involve my innermost feelings. Though I never regarded them as a waste of time since everyone is entitled to explore their talents. In the 1980's I used to write songs and other pieces which I couldn't identify what they were because I never felt the need to fit a melody to them, I just wanted these stanzas to be read. They were so special to me that I never wanted anybody to lay a hand on them or read them without my knowing. Then one day at a rehearsal, after I had become an actress, my stage manager and I were discussing what we did besides acting. I found out that he was also writing. I asked if I could bring my songs and other writings so that maybe he could define whether they were any good or not. When I handed them to him, he said, "okay, can you sing one of these songs?" After I had finished singing, he said "you know, the lyrics are good and so is the melody. That was a beautiful song." He took the other pages and began reading, but I could see from his expression that there was something wrong or missing. When he'd finished reading, he sat down with me and showed me how to go about it. He told me to keep on writing, that the work wasn't bad for a start. When I brought the second lot to him, he read them patiently, then said, "Bella, in poetry language we economise, you can do without some of these words." I asked him if what I was writing was poetry and he replied, "Bella, this is poetry." From then on I had more courage to write.

ALLAN KOLSKI HORWITZ: THE PROVINCE WRITES BACK (AN EXTRACT FROM AN INTERVIEW CONDUCTED BY DIRK KLOPPER)

DK: You have said that you oppose what you call "Colonial English", and that you want to sabotage it. Why do this to English and how do you propose to do this?

AKH: I would not use the term "sabotage"; it is inappropriate. I spoke of recognising the reality of our situation and agitating for the acceptance of our own unique forms of English. The recent controversy about the redefining of the English channel of Radio South Africa was very revealing. It showed just how strong the colonial impulse still is although English in South Africa is not "English" English - we have our own characteristic accents, vocabulary, images and preoccupations. The language doesn't belong to just the descendants of the English settlers. And in a more general sense English is now the lingua franca of most of Africa - in fact, of the world. So using English is to discourse in a world language which is being shaped by many cultures. In the same way that Latin or Arabic as imperial languages became lingua francas which retained their classical identity but then transformed into regional variants, so in South Africa, we have an original form of English which is very vital but which needs to be further developed and, above all, recognised. Though previously constrained by Apartheid and other colonial models, we now have an opportunity to assert this vitality. In any event, the Empire is long dead. So let us freely participate in a linguistic experiment which is adequate to the task of expressing our lives.

DK: Is this then a question of the "province" writing back to the metropolitan centre?

AKH: Firstly, I would say that most South Africans have never felt "at home" in the Empire - and have, in fact, resisted it whether from the African or the Boer perspective. Only a small minority has claimed a link with Britain. For most of us, the Empire represented tyranny and dispossession. If we are now "writing back", it is a sign that we are, at last, standing on our own feet - a sign of growing self confidence and independence. The pity has been that it has taken so long and that the colonials of all classes and colours in our society still consider "overseas" to be the final arbiter of standards and taste. This feeling of being inadequate and marginal, of being on the fringes, even though the global economic and information revolutions have swept away borders and realigned centres of influence, is the greatest obstacle to the flourishing of our own dynamic culture. In addition to the pathos of this position, what makes it so ironic is that today even New York, the centre of the American Empire, has lost its position as the international cultural capital. Literature, film, dance and the visual arts from all over the world are exchanged contemporaneously. The time has never been more opportune for South African voices to express themselves - not parochially, not chauvinistically, but in a self-fulfilling way to insist on our own experience.

DK: Even if we are using Tsotsi-taal to do so!

AKH: Absolutely! Although we know full well that Tsotsi-taal is not the only vehicle. However, as long as the intermingling of our languages and images is not taking place at the level of the social elites, we must look to the streets, shebeens, sports fields and jails where it is happening. Our rulers live in their security-walled ghettos so as to keep Africa at bay. By Africa, I mean the immediately local and particular, out of which will rise the authentic speech and rhythm of South African culture which will have universal significance. On the other hand, we should not be facile and think that using local languages automatically produces great poetry. No matter the language, poetry must satisfy several criteria: freshness, intensity, honesty, depth and technical excellence. In conclusion, it is our hope that the work of the Botsotso Jesters meets these demands.

IKE MBONENI MUILA : SOUL FOOD BINDER

From where I stand looking out of my life window pane, with no doubt I could definitely say everything started from inside, from the unknown to the obvious, from the obvious to the unknown. Almost everything that moves my soul next to the heart, a combination of music and poetry is not more or less the beginning of how I paved my way into creative writing or poetry as such. From 1988 to '89 I was at Funda Centre under the Soyikwa Institute of African Theatre for my stage drama diploma, I was approached by the Madimba music students for a music poetry performance at the library. I was asked to prepare a Venda poem. I had to explain before rehearsals what the poem was all about. Contemporary jazz music and poetry worked magical wonders for me in such a way that one could not draw a line between music and poetry in harmony. I mean, listen to people when they chat or deliver jokes using a combination of words from all different languages brought together without any fancy formalities. It stands to reason why at times one cannot just sit pondering and small wonder why people do not just eat dry mielie meal or chicken meat raw as it is without the feathers removed - one thing for sure, we need all the ingredients and necessary spices to make it meaty, juicy and tasty. In terms of language being food for the heart and soul - it is supposed to be substantial, thought provoking, funny and interesting - keeping your reader or audience intact.

Before I happily received my second stage drama diploma from the Market Theatre Laboratory, I had to frequently visit the then thought to be 'home for creative writers', COSAW. I used to watch videos in the COSAW library of the renowned poets, especially the one who used to move my soul next to the heart, and that one alone is amongst the works of Langston Hughes; "I have known rivers big and small".

My second stage drama diploma marked my turning point to the creative writing arena on a full time basis. People who had a lot of influence on me and my works in one way or another were, Lesego Rampolokeng and Siphiwe Ka Ngwenya, to mention but a few. Now that I am in command of my writing, I write what I like. I once wrote to Robert Berold, sending him a few of my creative writings. He sent me some guiding notes from a poetry discussion paper which was an eye opener, assisting me in many ways with my creative writing and style. By style I mean a kind of transparent combination of all the different languages that kept the people of South Africa separate for quite too long. I write Isicamtho, the so called Tsotsitaal Iringasi which is a township communication fire works lingo which differs from one place to another.

In a performance group and in this collaborative poetry writing with the Botsotso Jesters my work appears to be more than just creative writing, it becomes more of a poetry in motion.

ANNA VARNEY:
WHY THE WORKSHOP CONCEPT IS IMPORTANT

At workshops, a magical formula is activated. For one thing, there is a collective energy and creativity which is sparked off when a group of artists work closely together in an open way. Each participant contributing and interacting, both consciously and unconsciously, drawing from their own experience and perspective.

In 'normal circumstances' having to work together with others (who are often virtual strangers) would be stressful. But here a vitality is created, similar to rubbing flint stones together. Potentially negative energies are channelled into art-making if participants approach their work in an expansive and experimental manner.

Many artists initially approach workshops with scepticism, believing their individuality to be threatened by the collective situation. But an artist can't simply loose the sense of self and start working like his/her colleagues. Rather, something new is brought into the world. It is true that sometimes one leaves a workshop feeling unclear as to what it's effect was. But as the months go by, it is revealed in one's work. Fresh elements appear which were clearly sown at the workshop.

My first experiences took place in the realm of the visual arts. In 1987 I attended a one day drawing workshop at the Alex Arts Centre. In 1988 I attended my first Thupelo National Artists Workshop and in 1991 I attended the international Zimbabwean art workshop, Pachipamwe. In 1994 I joined the Botsotso Jesters.

In visual art workshops there are the demands and pressures of having a limited amount of time followed by an exhibition which takes place at the end. However, with the Botsotso Jesters, although we have had deadlines from time to time for performances or publications, we generally met on an ongoing basis until we were satisfied that a collective poem was coherent, original and appropriate.

South Africa emerges from a history of culture which has been severed and blocked rather than promoted and nurtured. Artists can only benefit, beyond all imagining, from the workshop concept. And obviously the broader the spectrum of participants, in terms of cultural background and individual modes of expression, the greater the reward for all -

>   this workshop I am not trying
>   to make wine out of water
>   - I am making wine
>   out of grapes
>
>   this workshop is like a hand
>   brushing over a surface
>   collecting a thin layer of dust
>   - it is like the gathering of that

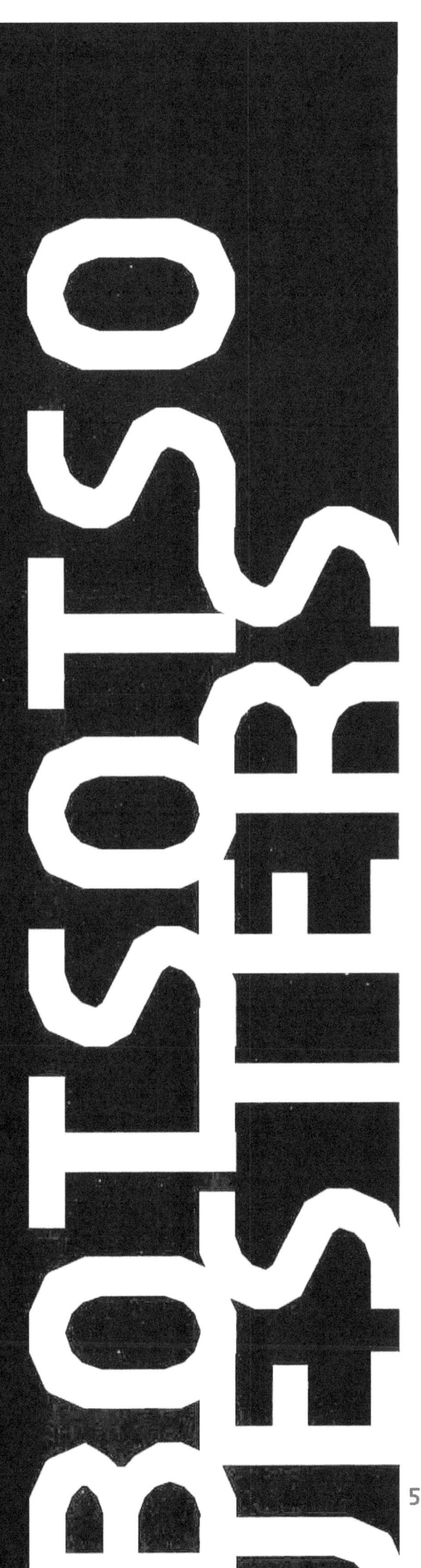

PART 1:

PERFORMANCE POETRY
COLLECTIVE WORKS BY
THE BOTSOTSO JESTERS:

IN THE LAND OF PLENTY	6
BOTSOTSO JESTERS	8
FREEDOM CHANTER	10

IN THE LAND

Cry of the silent scream
when prestige is for leaders
where blue lagoons serve causes
but the down-trodden are congested

in the land of plenty

dogs sniff breakfast food and branch
people exchange sex fun with robo corpse
ba bula donkey mapara and wild animals 1
children swap roles with their parents

in the land of plenty

winter veld ready for blackening
tinder-box set for lighting
at Bloemfontein, place of cheetahs
the dogs of Vlakplaas bark, no way

in the land of plenty

piles of fruit on a plate
tits, sex organs and other meat
drinks all round the table
come on sweetness, there's plenty to eat

in the land of plenty

a naked woman runs away
from a blasting time-bomb
in the streets of the golden city
like someone in a porno movie

in the land of plenty

TV shows roasting chicken rotating
the programme baking over a micro oven
man queues for a bus
in someone else's wardrobe

in the land of plenty

stretch up, blou van ons Azania
droughts only break when it pains here
suiping for too long at rivers of megalomania
now we wake babbelas

in the land of plenty

poems become forbidden fruit
fiery metaphors are buried
history becomes a mystery
devils lead saints to the pastures of sin

in the land of plenty

illusion mixers are concrete casspirs
nothing costs more than a funeral
mansion dwellers employ a Third Force
- who's that -

in the land of plenty

viva siya nqoba   2
viva now is the time
no strings attached
lucky strike right cords

in the land of plenty

candle light face of darkness
into Majuba hill mobile
from abc to xyz
city lights of Verwoerd tunnel

in the land of plenty

guns sing like bongos
lovers fake in response to fear
a charred corpse lies like a dog's carcass
in the warzones of Thokoza

OF PLENTY

in the land of plenty

now we've danced the toyi-toyi
dead folk become new spirits
"no strike" export zones employ Springbok
Patrols
to guard boss-investor visits

in the land of plenty

Bafana Bafana Amabokoboko
building the rainbow nation
steroid machines slaughter each other
global TV sweat sensation

in the land of plenty

slacks van ladies in mooi dorpie
brain glasses tinted decades ago
jy kom van swartkop
bowls of madness

in the land of plenty

Nofanezile Maria Masilela, aged 92,
says this about voting:
when I applied for my dompas, I made a cross
when I got married, I made another cross
and today I made what will probably be my last
cross

in the land of plenty

yesterday is a caricature
as we gather to celebrate dawn
is our future a mirage?
the revolution a pimpernel?

in the land of plenty

  1. to bugger a donkey
  2. we are winning

BOTSOTSO

(Poetic script for different characters)

ISABELLA: I am the light from the roof top
revealing fa ofa fi in your bed 1
barometer oiling screw hinges loose

SIPHIWE: Pensioner standing in a queue
ragged animals in the zoo
yawning toothless lions

ALLAN: I am fire burning the shack
smoking after the hostel attack
divide and rule is a problem here

IKE: Soul food binder stay free
silaphanje nge mum for men 2
eat your heart and lungs out

ANNA: Left over raped - sour grape
cooks rot in a pot
eats the whole damn lot

ISABELLA: Vumani bo siya vuma
thatha khotha thatha phuza thatha chatha 3
we are the healers from the sea

ALLAN: Stink of scam in the state
bureaucrat shuffle while you wait
nepotists scoop the honey

ANNA: The only hole god made
found my stomach today
- babbelas - cold forks - ash graves -

SIPHIWE: Listen to my voice at the shop door
listen as you walk to the sounds of war
umngena ndlini mama umngena ndlini baba

IKE: Stripper lelohembe asidlali
nkhetheni ke wa ponto le sheleng
sendela ngeno mujita ri vhonane 5

ISABELLA: Senkqanang se nthola morwalo
mpatle ka tiro tsame gotle butie
O seqe phefo ka nna legetleng 6

ALLAN: I'm the bull running the kraal
don't pull my ring if you're skraal
Sun City Extra

ANNA: The louse I'm serving tea to
addresses only my husband - he just
wants to speak to 'the Daddy of the House'

SIPHIWE: Shebeen tables black with booze
girls caress beards of their fathers
mothers bump and grind with their sons

JESTERS.

IKE: Hout kop petty crime is a taboo
           shame on you daaso a ni hembi 7
           guys ni hava nchumu jokes aside 8

ALLAN: Total Onslaught amnesty
           even Wit Wolf strolls out free
           forgive and forget history

ISABELLA: Don't be afraid say it loud
           come out strong and be yourself
           ke monyako mpulele hee 9

ANNA: I'm five years old, you're six foot tall
           teacher teacher tales of cancer
           beats my knuckles against the wall

SIPHIWE: Darkness shadow in the slums
           pockets cold with a stainless knife
           pass the bucks or I'll take your life

IKE: Ginger face butters no record to trace
           ready stomach digests sound of my words
           no bubble gum music in my verse

1. revealing give and take in your bed
2. we are here with mum for men
3. Do you agree?" "Yes I agree"
   "Take this and lick, take this and drink" (dialogue between Sangoma and patient)
4. small gift for those at home
5. Take off that shirt, we're not joking cheap boaster about money, come closer, let's see each other
6. If you no longer love me, then you relieve me, if you want to find me, look for me in my works, cut the wind with me on your shoulders
7. shame on you there, I am not lying
8. I'm not lying, guys I have nothing.
9. I'm at the door, open for me

FREEDOM CHANTER

In 1955 June 26
Tokologo was discussed 1
in 1994 April 26
she built herself a house
let live Tokologo
for the people shall govern

ginger man
force
shelela 2
tiekie line
hao tla 3
ka botlhale 4
you forget
ke bana ba haol 5

Tendani was born 6
in 1955 June 26
muukukulume 7
u tshi lila tendani 8
child abuse
shall be abolished
gauteng

with a handful of nails
boards from a shack
a platform was built
for the people's thoughts -
platform
to bear
weight and lightness

imagine a deep rooted tree
with laden branches spread out far
- whoever gathers from its fruit
plants still further seeds -
till there's an orchard
far as eyes can see

vultures overslept
woke up to find the freedom charter
coiled like a mamba
ready to strike
kliptown where people sang
the same tune
danced to the same rhythms

1. freedom
2. slip
3. when you come
4. with tricks
5. that they are your children
6. Venda persons name meaning 'one who has belief'
7. cock
8. Tendani is a proverb meaning 'belief'

10

THE PEOPLE SHALL GOVERN

Noha ya maraba 1
eho loma 2
e futhumetse 3
lodgers and stray people
in your backyard
govern
your yard
and your family
uzi donsele amanzi
ngo msele 4
the people shall govern
your husband
in your bedroom
ba rua dintja 5
le dikatse lebalengla hao 6
join the train
of ideas and bridge
the distance
for the people shall govern

1. cobra
2. bites you
3. when it feels hot
4. what you do back-fires
5. to keep dogs and cats
6. in your yard

ALL NATIONAL GROUPS SHALL HAVE EQUAL RIGHTS

all flowers and thorns
floods of rainbow petals
all peaches
sweetnesses to savour
all beasts
in flight

and each tribe makes its stay
fills graveyards
turns lies into history

food prepared	all tasty
gods worshiped	all holy
children born	all loved
law laid	all savage
	compassionate

then salt your bread
make this journey
under the Milky Way
care for the seed
of the one
mother and father

we can fight the world

why fight the world?
respect
be wise

THERE SHALL BE WORK AND SECURITY

Iron steel
workers bureau
bear my name
on the jobless
list above
for the office
bearer
of the jobless
people
for the people
by the people
themselves
Nzie i fhufha
nga doko
pity shame
when I turn
to a dustbin
of all assorted
jigsaw puzzle
junk food question
on my plate
murder violence
rape and plunder
orders of the day
alcohol anonymous
sewerage
hiccups blockade
mbila
yo kundwa Mutshila
ngo u rumela
Jeppe old boys
job cart
zabalaza
traffic germs
alter your ways

THERE SHALL BE WORK AND SECURITY (TRANSLATION)

Iron steel
workers bureau
bear my name
on the jobless
list above
for the office
bearer
of the jobless
people
for the people
by the people
themselves
the locust fly
with dung
pity shame
when I turn
to a dustbin
of all assorted
jigsaw puzzle
junk food question
on my plate
murder violence
rape and plunder
orders of the day
alcohol anonymous
sewerage
hiccups blockade
rock rabbit
is without a tail
Jeppe old boys
job cart
struggle
traffic germs
alter your ways

THE LAND SHALL BE SHARED
AMONG THOSE WHO WORK IT

when your work's so stony
your hands stay gashed
your back has an attack
slavery wrecks your feet

when you get the boot
you're sick and tired
the only hill you find to rest on
is owned
       by another Settler

when the light is frail
your inner landscape an escape
you sigh taking the tatty T-shirt
from your back:
"40 years hard labour
  yet
  I have nothing"

ALL SHALL ENJOY
EQUAL HUMAN RIGHTS

babies born addicted
stillborn
deflowered
drugs sell like popcorn
schools turned into holiday resorts
dens for gangster-lions

poets grace palaces
to get onboard
the gravy train
forget the pain
while job seekers get haunted
azikho lomsebenzi   no vacancy
bulldozers and police move the homeless
like amagoduka birds

santa claus dominates
tv
in the free state
satanists
gather round a candle
made of human fat
and african gods are grounded

ALL SHALL BE EQUAL BEFORE
THE LAW

You say
all shall be
equal before
the law?

you open an account
in a shebeen
wearing a torn
tattered
weary trouser
ordering
a hundred rand menu
at night you sleep
under the table
in a tin house
you say
all shall be
equal before
the law
u hluba ama peanuts   1
eating chips
van goedgedagte
you say
I don't eat potatoes
you say
all shall be
equality
before the law

1. to boast about something small

THE PEOPLE SHALL SHARE IN THE COUNTRY'S WEALTH

foot wears
one shoe
mouth chews
one mouthful
choir sings
one song at a time

in shop windows
faces of many things
smile and beckon -
hungry people stare

and those who know -
bread baked for stomachs
clothes woven to warm nakedness
shelters built against lightening
arts and sciences
magic meaning

say   why   Anglo trillions
    why   Sanlam billions
why   Rembrandt millions

when we people
live under the same sun
on the same earth
drinking from the same rivers

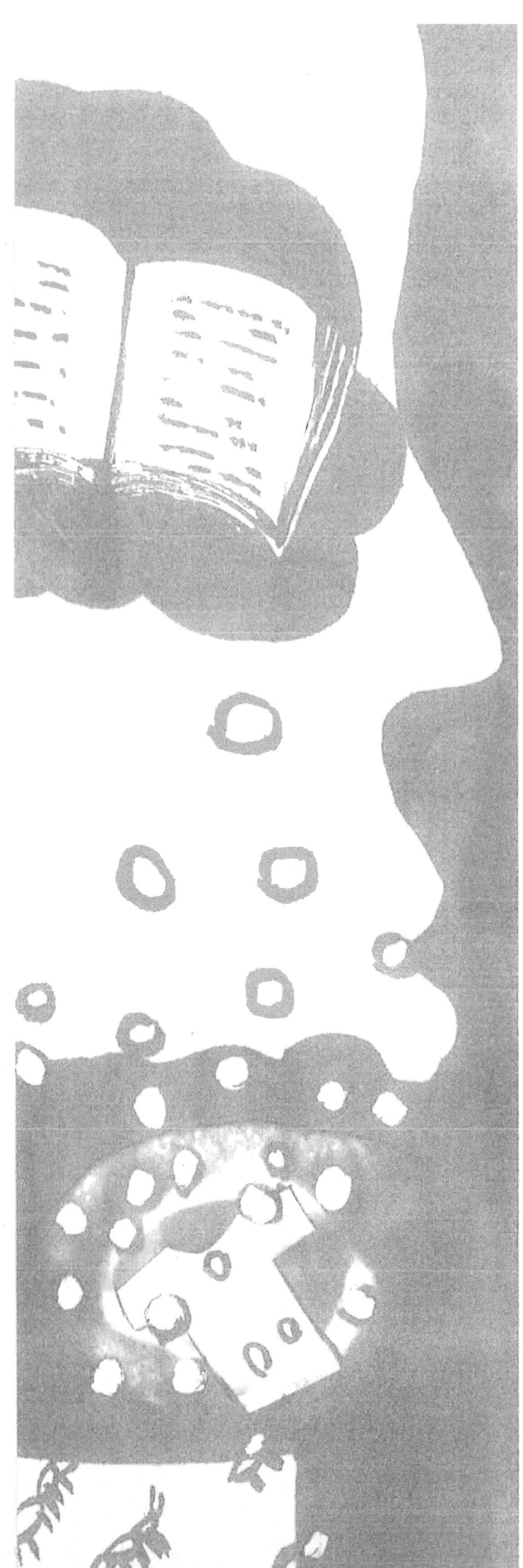

THE DOORS OF CULTURE AND LEARNING SHALL BE OPENED

bookworms
red ants trust
aliens
meet to exchange ideas
for the doors
shall be open-ended
washing powder
of ideas
shall follow suit
open up
changing rooms
wa wyde
teach youth phadisano   1
to love
liberty na mulalo   2
human brotherhood
khuliso ngeno   3
education
become our cultural custom

1. competition
2. and peace
3. honour here

THERE SHALL BE HOUSES
SECURITY AND COMFORT

day's light still lingers
the yellow bird's perched on the gate
and bees all over
the cornflower coloured tree

I close the curtains
on a sacred sky

   that's why houses had better be special
 - what shuts out the sky
   had better be special

let's build modest dwellings
show reverence to the vessel
which holds us
let's have no more palaces
or things guarded by such walls
which mean:
    g a i n f o r f e w
    l o s s f o r a l l

THERE SHALL BE PEACE AND FRIENDSHIP

my pockets full of
holes
pots full of boiling water
inside my fridge
nothing to ease
your babbalas

i fight cockroaches
for crumbs
and friends fade like salt in
water

in my heart
i want to compose poems about
flowers that do not wither

a woman cries in the night
her voice drowned
by a bellowing gumba gumba
the law arrives late
like a late night movie

warriors chant usuthu
raising the spirit of shaka zulu
and like streams of the same river
we hoist a rainbow flag
singing
nkosi sikelela die stem morena boloka
someone in a car raises the middle finger
and in parliament they dance the
rdp tango

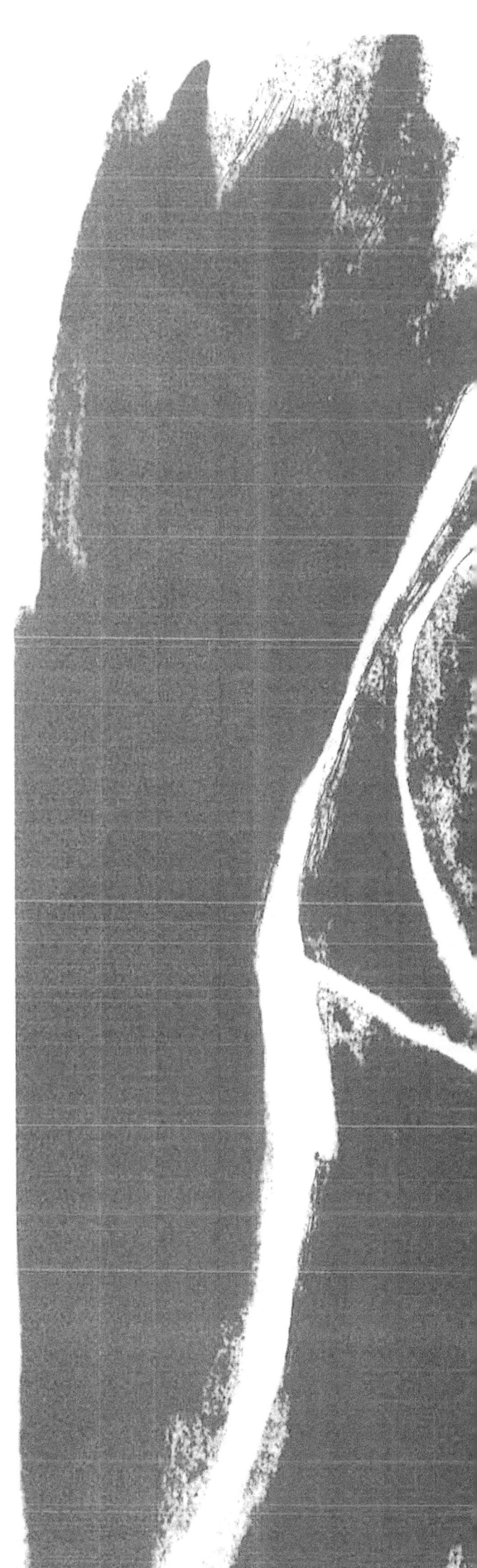

FREEDOM SHUNTED

it's the year 2995
and there's a museum called:
"Products of the Old South Africa"
in it hangs the Freedom Charter
which speaks of The Brotherhood
and a dream for all human beings
in those days of racism, sexism
and every kind of oppression
they did things like that -
put golden promises onto papers
which yellowed from age and lack of use

our leaders sat with the crocodile
and came away with their lives
more than that
they said they came away
with a way for all the people
they came back with constitutions and
programs for making the land
competitive
don't make demands
ask - what can I contribute?
our leaders sat with the crocodile
government is slow very slow
chewing with the crocodile

jy vat en sit
no money for lobola
mixed marriage is what you call
equality before the law?

mudryseni school dungaree 1
in a Soweto taxi rank
children born HIV positive
ndi saga dza nnyi 2
work and security
read the robot
head over tail
vhukalanga ndi ngafhi 3
nwananga 4
urine marks
white pepper survival
at large
standing alone
shakarha mina 5
where is your beacon
big willie tumbles
hamburger for ejaculation

yes, at kliptown
you carried our ivory dreams
freedom charter
like a praying mantis
you swallowed your victims

1. driver
2. whose responsibility
3. where is the north
4. my child
5. my relative

PART 2:

DUETS:
IKE MBONENI MUILA
AND ISABELLA MOTADINYANE

VULANI	21
BONANG WEE	22

COLLABORATIONS:
ALLAN KOLSKI HORWITZ
AND ANNA VARNEY

RINGMAN	23
SALT	24

VULANI [1]

Zizo buya iinkomo
Zizo buya iinkomo zika baba
Kudala silindile
Silindile iinkomo zika baba
Muilisa wandele mathakha
Zibuyile iinkomo zika baba
Bramanie na Mashango
Dzo orowa
Kudala silindile
Silindile iinkomo zika baba
Vulani amasango
Zibuyile iinkomo zika baba

OPEN UP (TRANSLATION)

The cows will return
my father's cows will return
it has been a long time
waiting for my father's cows
honest herdsman
in the grazing field
my father's cows are back
Bramanie na Mashango [2]
returns home
it has been a long time
waiting for my father's cows
open up the gates
my father's cows are back home

1. Vulani is a song about a herdboy who went to collect cattle from the grazing field. The people at home complain about having to wait so long. But being a trustworthy herdboy he does bring all their cattle home, calling from the distance that they must open up the kraal - all his father's cattle are returning.
2. names of cows

BONANG WEE [1]

Bonang wee
Bonang iyoo

One for sorry
Two for joy
Three for coming
Six for kiss
Four for meet
Eight for money

We go places
We meet faces
All over the world

Bonang wee
Bonang iyoo

Lapeng la heso ho tsikitlano ya meno
Lapeng la heso ho koduo ya maseru
Ha ho ngwana ya motle ditjabeng

One for sorry
Two for joy
Three for coming
Six for kiss
Four for meet
Eight for money

Bonang wee
Bonang iyoo

A CRY OF COME AND SEE (TRANSLATION)

A cry of come and see
A cry of come and see

One for sorry
Two for joy
Three for coming
Six for kiss
Four for meet
Eight for money

We go places
We meet faces
All over the world

A cry of come and see
A cry of come and see

Our home is a home
Of tears and bitterness
Our home is a home
Of crisis

There is no
Beautiful child
Of the nation

One for sorry
Two for joy
Three for coming
Six for kiss
Four for meet
Eight for money

A cry of come and see
A cry of come and see

1. Bonang Wee is a song about doves flying in the open sky and their meaningful signs to us. When two doves appear your way, it is believed that lots of joy is due to you. If it is seven doves that you see, you're going to receive a letter or message. (How does this compare with the horoscope!)

RINGMAN

ringman ringeye
tell me
how do you fare?
I see you walk all over
Rissik street
for a loaf of rye
people stare at your eye
pretend you're not there
you try Jeppe
President Main Kerk Kruis
it all gets you nowhere
just the same everywhere

just the same
they stare if they dare
at the void round
your orb
black/purple mark
of the dark
ringman knowman
your cold hole in which
you stitch the world's web
arm with the axe
leg with the lopped
off knee

you parade to be free
ringman
circling
the pooled
smooth face
of tears
in your irisless eye
how you try to defy
the lie
of the spy

ringman you know
the sum of all equations
is zero
nowhere from here
it's all done
the eye stares
inward and outward
you stop on Rissik
they think you're in a coma
bombed and bruised
they still pretend
you're not there

but you're all in a lotus!

SALT

Snoek thrown
from small boats onto the quay
red gashes
behind their gills
silver   long
dead snoek

for salting frying smoking

smack of dead snoek on the quay
boats crammed with scales
men in thick jerseys
haul the silver
smack/smack on the quay

our hands clasp in the breeze
seven shades of blue
cross the ocean face
violet purple azure aquamarine
turquoise cobalt and lapis lazuli

depth of water
shades
reflecting

stepping through twin rainbows
double sign
of a turning point to come
lifting tortoises over the road
so they may never be crushed
then another omen
reminds us to regard
the slow but unwavering

great burnt moon
following us home
dimming over Atlantis
because none should linger there
none to reveal the gannets beak
skimming the surface
smack-smack of snoek on the quay

you are the second skin
the penultimate idea
the next breath I take
each harbour town each Karoo town
slow cerise skies
exterior reflections of another
landscape we share

and in the one star hotel
with the matador painting
fishcakes for lunch
we pour wine from bottles
abandoned at twelve

you collect shells on the beach
to place on the steps
of our front door one
thousand kilometres inland
but still washed by currents
tang of salt
cooking the snoek
smack-smack
scales on the quay

PART 3:

POEMS BY SIPHIWE KA NGWENYA:

WE JIVE LIKE THIS	26
KLIPTOWN SHANTYTOWN	27
RETRENCHMENT	27
DANCE AFRICA	27
UKUSHONA KWELANGA	28
SUFFOCATION	28
WHEN IT RAINS	29
SEE YOU IN ANOTHER LIFE	29
MELODY FOR MBONENI WANGU MUILA	30
MELODY FOR MAMASE	30
MELODY OF WAITING	30
NATURAL INITIATION	31
POET	32
FUNERAL	32
OBSESSED	33
ACHIEVEMENTS	33
CANDLELIGHT	34
LET ME SING A SONG	35
MELODY TO MELODY	36

WE JIVE LIKE THIS

like foetus dancing inside the womb
in haste to scrutinise the world
    we jive like this
    we jive like this
    we jive like this
like babies lullabyed by screams of martyrs
silenced by furious fangs of freedom's satires
    we jive like this
    we jive like this
    we jive like this
like youth burning with desire of wisdom
denied by the bully bullet's beats of boredom
    we jive like this
    we jive like this
    we jive like this
like workers trampling on the master's religion
of divide and rule's tampering mission
    we jive like this
    we jive like this
    we jive like this
like god's followers dancing to the drumming whip
for the sins sown but never reaped
    we jive like this
    we jive like this
    we jive like this
like soldiers with rifles and flowers raised to the
sky
when marching to the ecstasies of twisted victory
    we jive like this
    we jive like this
    we jive like this
like lion and tiger embracing each other
forced to forge a painful togetherness
    we jive like this
    we jive like this
    we jive like this
like the god's sangomas around clouds of incense
in a trance to foretell a future that isn't only roses
ah
our feet jump like springboks when stamping
    when we jive like this
our knees are not sagging
    when we jive like this
    when we dance our jive

    we jive like this
    we jive like this
    not like that
    we jive like this
    like this
    like this

KLIPTOWN SHANTYTOWN
(1 NOVEMBER 1994)

kliptown shantytown
dreams silenced
by the morning train
footsteps of running commuters

kliptown shantytown
the sky loses its brains
in torrents it starts to rain
people use tables as boats

kliptown shantytown
when day is young
women wash clothes down the river
children swim like fish in dirt

kliptown shantytown
factory machines cease
workers return home like cattle
to ghetto smoke and kisses of longing

kliptown shantytown
frogs croak crickets chirp children snore
and nakedness entangles with passion
till dawn

RETRENCHMENT
(30 SEPTEMBER 1994)

sacrificial lambs
we sat in their boardroom
tea and coffee
silver pots and tray
the employers banging the doors
in our faces
i hold tight
i with a yearning to be a child
never pierced by the thorny sides
of a rose
now i cannot sleep
i like someone dying
slowly
eaten alive by a virus

DANCE AFRICA

dance   africa
dance
dance   ejaculating freedom
dance   echelons of faith
dance   lions roaring in silence
dance   in a revolutionary stance
dance
dance   an epic in your hair
dance   fruitful dreams in your mind
dance   a kaleidoscope of memories
             memories
                for you africa
dance   dance eyes of a future we can find
dance   outrage and despair in your face
dance   tides of time on your lips
dance   twinkling stars in your heart
dance   clapping waste of liberation
             in copulation
dance   your never bending knees
dance   to marabi blues
dance   the toyi toyi dance
dance   rivonia
dance   boipatong
dance   bisho
dance   the embrace of impatience
dance   roaring passion of the sea
dance   serenades of stifled love
dance   colourful rainbow on the groove
dance   seeds of painful birth
dance   throbbing drums of the gods
dance   melody
             melody of our last harvest
dance   to mutabaraka's drug culture
dance   to lkj's dread beat 'n blood
dance   to oku onoura's ak47
dance   to clifton joseph
dance   to judy radul
dance   to rampolokeng's horns for hondo
dance   jayne cortez no compromising voice
dance   in a tapestry of victory
dance
dance

UKUSHONA KWELANGA

uma ilanga lishona
izinkomo sezibuyela esibayeni
sekungasazwakali nokuhlabelela kwezinyoni
phezulu esibhakabhakeni
izintombi zizinhle zicwebezela
amasoka ehamba lukeke
okwelanga lasebusika
mina ngimile ngincike esangweni
ngivaleke amehlo
ngisho ngiphelelwe nayinhliziyo
nengqondo yami igabadule izinkalo
uma sengikhumbule wena sthandwa sami
uma ilanga lishona

SUNSET
(TRANSLATION)

when the sun sets
cattle return to their kraal
and we no more hear
the singing of birds
in the sky
young women being beautiful
and shining
like winter sun
their suitors walk askant
i stand
leaning on the gate
eyes turning blind
becoming heartless
my mind gallops on the ridges
i long for you
my love
when the sun sets

SUFFOCATION

i wish
i could lock you inside a room
where no flowers bloom
with no ventilation to feel
the aromatic smell of air
leave you alone with a burning tyre
that you light out in the streets
while jesting over a zol of dagga
or breaking into song
over the inflamed breakdancing body
of an alleged witch
leave you alone with a cigar
that you puff trying to display your superiority
or erase torment in your mind
leave you alone with smoking grass
that irritates you with its winter dryness
or when trying to catch rodents in the veld
leave you alone with burning incense
watch you dance in the clouds
when exorsizing or psyching yourself
so i could watch you
choke
sneeze
cough blood
tears augmenting
your nose running
till you wet your pants
and scream
H E L P

WHEN IT RAINS

in the rural areas
where my ancestors are buried
people still rise
to the cock's crow
in the morning
young boys are shepherds
worshipping the sun
the moon, the stars
virgins walk proudly
they are the custodians of youth

when it rains
after a long drought
the people beat drums
leaving empty buckets outside
children sing and dance
for the rivers shall overflow
the pastures shall be green
anguish will be mere history
and the people shall harvest
the sweat of their toil

SEE YOU IN ANOTHER LIFE

some would-be ghosts
have tasted bitterness
of the earth
which
like a glutton
has swallowed
many loved ones

somewhere in the dark
they who yearn to be free
hope to meet in spirit
in paradise
where no one returns from
to tell a tale
they hold hands and take an oath
dousing themselves in petrol
flames of fire dance
as they burn

we who remain
overwhelm life

MELODY FOR MBONENI WANGU MUILA

wasekaya
tell me
when those ngulube spies
in the bright lights
of embiza
in front of the ccv's of ejozi
three star okapis in their hands
vertel my gazi
my ma se kind
never did you think
of reciting for them a poem
net a bietjie van isicamtho
to resist those okapis
from penetrating your body
forcing you to dance
kofifi style
a dance jy sal never nie forget
until the muilas come
to possess you

MELODY FOR MAMASE

when i look at you
you bring to me
sad memories
tears
tears i once shed for my mother
when she left me on this earth
and i had to fend for myself
while i was still crawling
to life
you have grown up now
you know why i hide my poems
against those men
with crunching boots
honky tonks
and dangling guns

MELODY OF WAITING

tired
of waiting
and just waiting
(for freedom to come
knock at our doors?)
now that our candles are on the ready
against rotten waiting
genocide
how long
this melody
that squeezes me like an orange
a tin shack
a waterpipe
a pavement
a dingy park
when there is plenty of land
tired
of waiting for this train
this melody
tired

NATURAL INITIATION

while other
would-be men
trudge the bushes
of the mountain tip
to be circumsized and
advised
by their elders
who know the thorny
road of life

you
woman
circumsized me
with the bitter
sweet taste of my blood
drawing images
on our lovebed
words whispered
shining
with compassion
into my ears
sinking in my heart
deeper than
the monotonous verse
of the initiator

so when i walked again
where my feet walked
many years gone by
i could feel you
and i was born again
crowing of cocks
bleating of sheep
bellowing of bulls
birds singing on trees

when the sky's tears
began to fall
thinking
alone in my room
searching deep
joyful memories
came to haunt me
my rooted past
i saw you coming
real
only fate setting us apart
i resisted an ocean
welling in my eyes

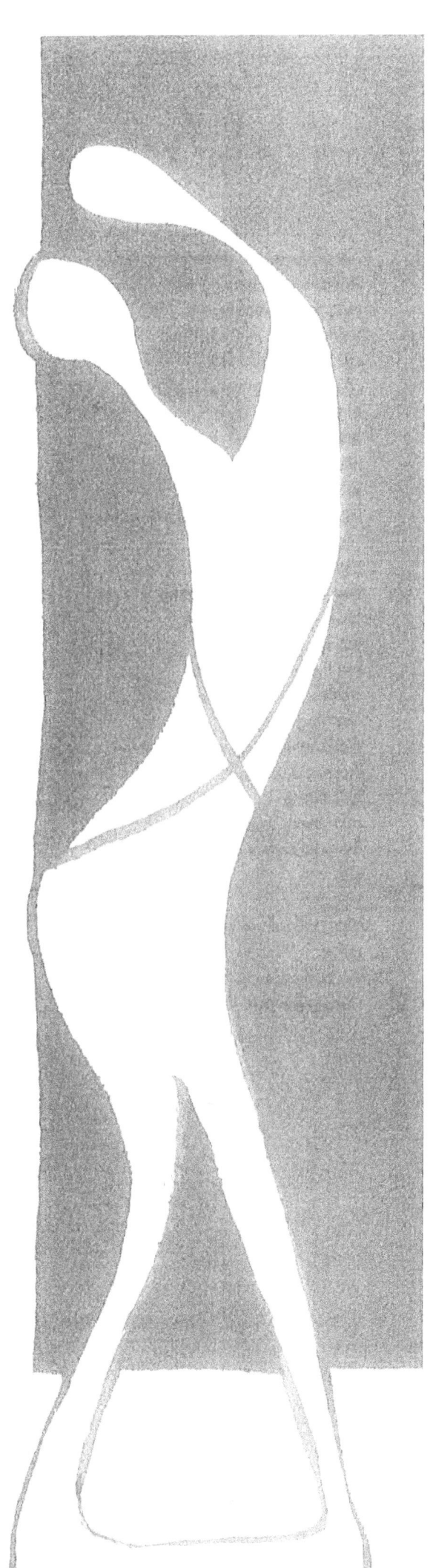

POET

a poet jumps on stage
like someone running away from a mob
goes to the microphone
holds it
caresses it like a baby
coughs to clear out the phlegm
in the throat
adjusts the tone
like a lover on the phone
looks at the audience
like a king or queen looks at subjects
 - ants
check one - two
then the voice reverberates
blowing every eardrum
flowers bloom
but the future is gloom
rhythm pulsates like sea waves
cracking on rocks
theme sinks deep inside the mind
there is a clamour
feet dance
after every poem
the poet orders another drink
sips
staggers
trips and falls to the ground
pukes
the audience rises
stoning the poet to death

FUNERAL

a limousine hearse purrs like a cat
comes to a halt
we give it right of way
a guard of honour
for the deceased inside a casket
stunned eyes feast
tears fall
putco buses rattle
tyres screech
car swerves
church songs lead the way to Avalon Cemetery
women in mini wrap-around jean skirts
super-curled hair
men festooned in golden jewellery
minding their own business
the coffin is lowered down the grave
tears fall on make-up
gun salutes
amidst whistling and ululation
we return to the deceased's home
wash our hands
indulge in salads
sweets and booze

OBSESSED

i wake every morning
from dreamless nights
see your silhouette
brightening the room of my mind

without you i die many deaths
i live with a piercing pain
of not revealing to you how my heart pounds
because fate chains my lips

how i cherish those moments
of warm hands clasping
fingers caressing and interlacing
and the sensuous elevating voice

i always wish the embrace would last longer
everytime we reach out to kiss goodbye
so i could see the glow in you
and the questioning in your eyes

i always wish i could look at you
beyond a sprout of desire
since you censored the moistness of sucking lips
but still cannot hold back
for you capture me like a mimosa
without you i am void of life

ACHIEVEMENTS

black faces mouthing slogans
toilets before houses
free service at clinics
bread & peanut butter
and milk for the poor
cheap labour for the jobless
tin shacks growing everywhere like mushrooms
blood on every front page
and a cry of outrage

CANDLELIGHT

i yearn for you
caress and smell the sweet scent of your breath
but we are mountains divided
by an overflowing river

my eye can travel beyond
see the chocolateness
ebonyness of your glowing face
i wish i could wrap the hands of my poem
round your waist-bountiful
feel the warmth of your sturdy legs
but the river between us is deep

you overwhelm me with the softness
the boldness of your voice
like drumbeats it reverberates in my ears
how can i feel the rhythm of your heart
the drizzle of sweat on your bosom
when reality keeps us apart

when i am feeling
lonely and forsaken
your eyes brighten my path like a candle
making my heart leap
for you lift me from melancholy
to rapture

LET ME SING A SONG

let me sing a song
a song for mothers
their children swallowed in a
political harvest

let me sing a song
a song for daughters
their virginity stolen
by power-hungry maniacs

let me sing a song
a song for stalwarts
for shaking prison walls
breaking prison chains

let me sing a song
a song for children
whose anger and haste
cannot be measured or bulldozed

let me sing a song
a song for workers
who braved themselves
from darkness till darkness

let me sing a song
a song for my beloved
who stole my heart
forcing me to sweat

let me sing a song
a song for my people
who moved me into poetry
making it poetry of harassment

let me sing a song
a long forgotten song
a long forgotten ancient song
commanding us to rise

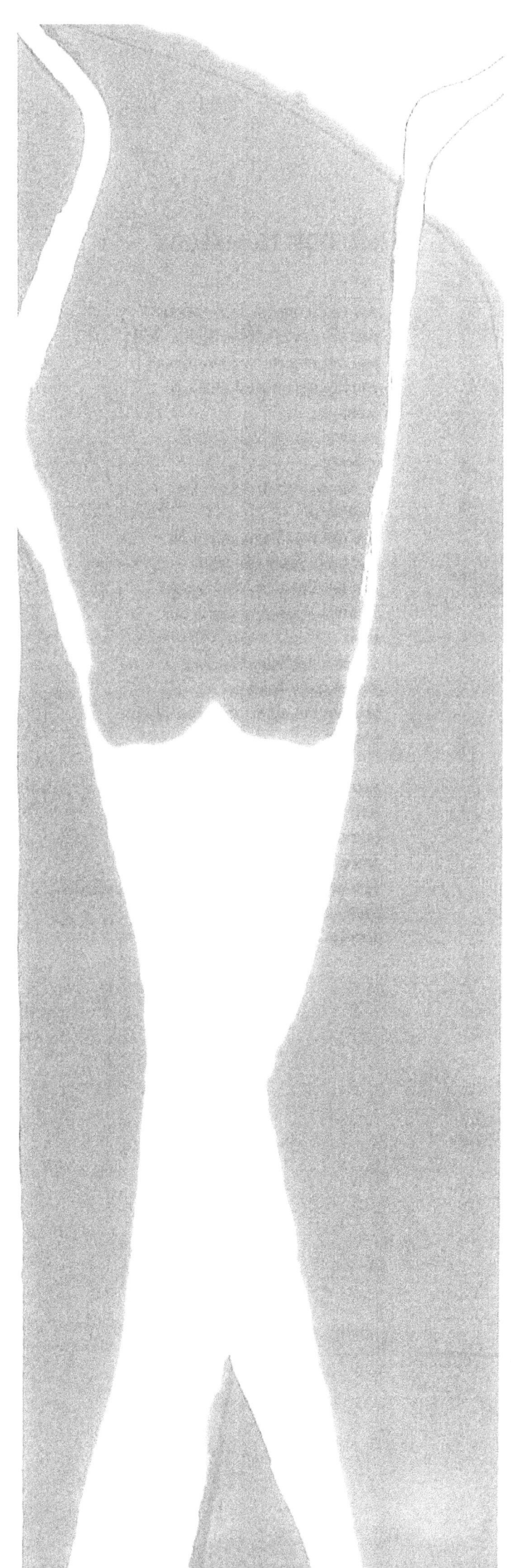

MELODY TO MELODY

you are a melody to a melody
you are a world beyond the world
you are unique and not eunuch
you are hips shaking life's ill
humours
you are the guiding light for
initiates
on the way to and from the
mountains
you are mountains which all
humanity yearns to climb
you are the rivers and oceans
where we yearn to bathe our
souls
you are the feared bushes
where guerrillas hide
you are the earth where nature
nurtures
      fruits of freedom
you are the tapping rain ripening
fruits to reap
you are Mandela's everlasting
smile on a Monday blues
you are a fast rhythm of talking drumbeats
soothing our ancient
sorrow

you are a womb labouring a
healthy baby
after listening to the deafening echoes
      of rat-a-tat-tat
you are the cold winds of
change blowing
in the morning when we
stampede like cattle to work
you are a lion roaring defiance
for equal rights
you are the whistling whispers
of sweat
when nude bodies of lovers bob
and weave
you are the ejaculation of a
people's long-lost liberty
you are an exodus to an epic
that i lack for your melody
because you are a melody to a
melody
you are melodies to melodies
melodies . . .

PART 4:

POEMS AND LYRICS BY ISABELLA MOTADINYANE:

TOUTING TAXI	38
TLONG BESO*	39
SINK A SHAFT	39
HOSHE NGWANA *	40
THOKOZANI **	41
STELLA	42
TELEVISION	42
TLOPO KGUBEDU*	43
ROPE SA MOTSWETSE*	44
ONE LEG IN	45
WHITE LACE	46
NONHLANHLA	46
RIBBON HANDS	47
WORK SHIRE	48
MR BROWN	48
PUSH ASIDE SQUEAKY	49

* translated by
  Ike Mboneni Muila
** translated by Ike Mboneni Muila and
  Isabella Motadinyane

TOUTING TAXI

Touting taxi
topsy
turvey
pep talk
from Zola
to Jozi
music background
loud and loud
pep talk
trace
toilet tissue
tracks
van bo
ke bona dibono 1
ke sa bone 2
beng ba tsona 3
taxi
topsy turvey
pep talk
constant thuggery
criss cross
cross pollination
Christianity charged
shot cut corner
Magomosha style 4
corner
Market and Nugget
taxi topsy
turvey
pep talk
drinking beefeaters
eyes off
melting bazookas
meaty juice
ba harela jwala 5
eke ba kgaohile maoto 6
kwala molomo lovey 7
ke mametse 8
touting taxi
topsy turvey
pep talk

1. I see buttocks
2. before I see
3. their owner
4. thuggery - name of a gang
5. drinking heavily
6. as if legs are broken
7. close your mouth lovey
8. I'm listening to

TLONG BESO

Paaha
tlong beso
paaha
tlong beso
ke nako ya ho hlaola
ke nako ya kotulo
tlong re buisaneng
tlong ka kutlwano
paaha
tlong beso
paaha
tlong beso
selemo se thwasitse
mabele a hodile
na le utlwile na
taba ketse monate
paaha
tlong beso
paaha
tlong beso

COME PEOPLE (TRANSLATION)

*Paaha
come people
paaha
come people
it is time to do away with weeds
it is time for the harvest
come let us talk
come in peace
paaha
come people
paaha
come people
it is summer time
the corncob is mature and ripe
have you ever heard
news of happiness?*

SINK A SHAFT

Dark night babe
toss and turn
the clouds above
you make the sober go drunk
come in from the cold
warm you up
sink down our throat
the clouds above
mountain so high
sink babe sink
sink a shaft
move slowly down the mountain
down our throats
toss and turn babe
sink on me
all night
in dark nights clouds above
you make the sober go drunk
sink babe sink
sink it smooth
sink a shaft

HOSHE NGWANA

Hoshe ngwana
qata o qatoge
melodi kafa le fa
ngwana dilkoti marameng
pososelo eka naledi
sefahleho sone
botjhitja bo kqahlang mahlo
re bone mesebetsi ya hao
naheng mona
ba reng
o sekobo
ke baikaketsi
ba lese ba iphore jaalo
shine bright sunbeam
hoha
kana wena o motswa mantlha
qata o qatoge thope
shine bright sunbeam
hoshe thope
hoha
moo o fetileng
ho sala dinaledi
thebetha mohlakwana
thebetha mofokeng
re bone mesebetsi ya hao
digaboi di tseleng jwale
raak hulle dizzy ousie
slaat hulle giddy poppy
ba fehlile jwale
ba ho bapallang sax

HUSH BABE (TRANSLATION)

Hush babe
walk tall
whistles here and there
smiling like a star
with a round face
dimple cheeks babe
that capture the eye
we saw your works here
in the country
those who say
you are ugly
they are liars
let them cheat themselves
shine bright sunbeam
ho ha
hush babe
by the way
you are number one
walk tall babe
shine bright sunbeam
hush babe
ho ha
where you left
you leave stars behind
tick talk mohlakwana clan
tick talk mofokeng clan
we saw your works
wedding presents now
are on the way
sister make them dizzy
make them giddy doll
they have arrived now
those who play sax for you

THOKOZANI

Open doors wide
for fresh air
seisi pelo magoletsa 1
Phefeni knows Mmabatho 2
Mofolo bare ke mmabona 3
hayani she stays 4
here she packs
there she goes
banthati ba kana ka banthoi 5
the villagers
and neighbours chuck me
no water to drink
no food to eat
shelter see to finish
no sunshine for me
God gives
God takes
He take all
for us who care
no beards to caress
nor lamb to lullaby
countless souls hate her
a pound of flesh suffers
no peace of mind
bricks break
thoughts free
tshingandededze 6
ba ithobaletseng 7
she kneels down
hand in hand
ntsu snuff
thokozani
she cried re utlwile phothuloha 8
o seke wa tshwenyeha 9
voices cry deeper
in black berry night
pillow rocks for
vivid apparition
white cloth
red beads
seisi pelo magoletsa 10
Thokozani

1. don't worry
2. names of places
3. they say it's their mother
4. home
5. who hate me are equal to those who love me
6. veins keep me moving
7. those who passed away
8. be free, we've heard
9. do not worry
10. do not worry

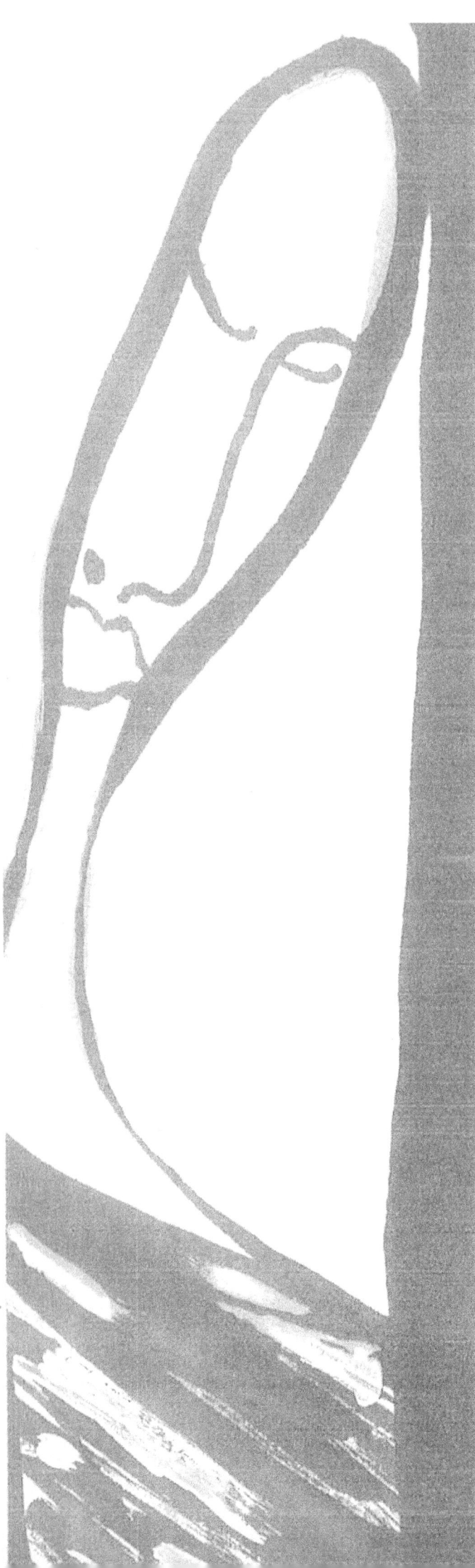

STELLA *

Stella Stella
I've been to your home
I found your mama there
She said
You left long ago
I saw tears in her eyes
And I knew
It was real
Stella come home
To me
Stella Stella
There is no life without you
Our kids are missing you
You know
I love you so
Come back
Stella Stella
Stella please come home
I've been to your home
I found your mama there
She said
You left long ago
Left her sick
And hungry

TELEVISION

In my dreams
tell a vision
you sitting on the loo
red lips
chewing gums
smoking cigarettes
between your fingers
your eyes see
a central line
in a vision
of my dreams
cats can pass

* lyric of a song

TLOPO KGUBEDU

Bonang wee
bonang yoo
lapeng la heso
ho tsikitlano ya meno
basadi ba kgelella dikeledi
bosiu le motshehare
tlopo kgubedi
kgoho e ntsho e kene
lapeng la heso
ngwana mme ntate
e qadile ka ntja ka ntle
a kobotile ho fihla leseeng
bonang wee
bonang yoo
re tla bona re entse
jwang na
thepa e ile yohle
re fuma keledi tsa
mosadi ka tlung
mme wee ese ele pina

RED HELMET
(TRANSLATION)

A cry
of come and see
a cry of
come and see
our home is a home
of tears and bitterness
women crying
night and day
a black cockerel
red helmet
is in the house
a smash hit
mother father child
ending up with
an infant
it started
with a dog outside
a cry
of come and see
what can we do now
household and furniture
everything is gone
we found a woman
in tears inside
a crying mother
is now a song

ROPE SA MOTSWETSE

Basadi matlung
banna ntle
ho qaaka mona
banna akqelang
pelo ya morena
melamu lese e lebale
phala dibe ho lona
ho qaaka mona
Mosadi atswa a kqenne
a jele sekaja
Fubu dile moyeng
mose a kuketswe dinokeng
Monna qosheletsaneng
tedu hase tsa botsofe
tedu ke tsa lekauta
Mosadi wa chobolo
o lebisitse bohale lekauteng
la hloka ho tsotella
la tswela pele le peipi
Phate tsa lahleha motseng
tjhaba sa hloka kqotso
Fanang beso
fanang ka tlotla
fanang ka kqotso
fanang ka rope sa motswete
le ahe kqotso motseng
Morena hlwella dithaba
O kope kqotso ho ramasedi
aho sedimotsetse
Rapedisa pula morena
kgomo tsa ntate
di shwele ke lenyora
baahisane haba mahlong
ba hadiketswe
dithotse melomong
metsi ha hosa kgellanwa
tsena ditaba di mahlong

MAIDENS THIGHS (TRANSLATION)

Women indoors
men outdoors
here lies the problem
men protect the chief's heart
do not forget traditional sticks
let the blowing horns
be by your side
here lies the problem
a woman appears sad
running and hungry
breasts in the air
dresses lifted below the wells
man in hide out
beards are not for aging
beards are for manhood
a fierce woman
directs her anger
to the bachelor
man loses his patience
he goes on
smoking his pipe
blankets go missing at home
national peace at stake
give one to another fellow men
give each to the other with pride
give to each other in peace
give one another a maiden's blanket
bring peace at home
survey the mountains Lord
ask for peace from the Almighty
to bring light to you
pray for rain my lord
my father's cattle
are dying of drought
neighbours are not ashamed
they are at loggerheads
they do not come
to each other's assistance
this is bad news

ONE LEG IN

One leg in
another leg out
tight me up
strongly sewn
visible mending
back pocket trademark
silver buttons attached
not woven once
twice or thrice
die is mos botsotsos   1
back pocket
front pocket
nog 'n maal talk to me
die is mos botsotsos
pull high
stretch on a high way
ons pedestry moet doves   2
no attention to whistlers my weebit
no hearing sweet nothings
strongly sewn
die is mos botsotsos

1. jeans made from stretch denim
2. we are pedestrians with doves

WHITE LACE

White lace
darkens voices
your scarface
calls
at a distance
Shwele baba 1
Shwele nkosi yami 2
children send you
to and fro
the world eats grass baba
people chew sorgum beer
you're lying on the ground
no pocket money
no bread
brown musk overall
bloodstained
danger races outdoors
Shwele baba
Shwele nkosi yami
Hail the King
Hail our great
Nomandumbuluzane 3

NONHLANHLA

Nonhlanhla is gone
tears pearls laughter
dreads survey my toes
touch of anguish
pat my mind
the target is found
Nonhlanhla is gone
They nailed her
pink nails oozing
they dragged her
reshuffled her
off the ground
pinned her tongue
hanging loose
blood pool flooded
to dry up heavens
Nonhlanhla is gone
Staring
into the dark
tired of nkosi yami
go away
biting my lips
my dark room walls
caressing the belt
to end the beginning
of a far away song
in my mind
Zion bells ring
bayavuya 4
umoya wami 5
uyakhathazeka 6
voices crying
in the dark
darkness
swallows the light
my heart
has stopped beating
no mercy in Zion
Nonhlanhla is gone

1. please father
2. please my Lord
3. seedlings
4. they are happy
5. my soul
6. is troubled

RIBBON HANDS

Ribbon hands
mama's little darling
matsoho ke dikgabisa
o botswa hore ha hole tjena
ja boi a tjhetjhe
nkane e bonala phatleng
bana ke dikgutsana
mmabo asaja mabele
hoseng oya mosebetsing
seeta sea hatwa hle
manala haa hloke pente
makgoa a motseba ele
Mrs so and so
kajeno nyalo e fedile
a dula marao jarateng
tsabo masterns
roll on
mabhobodlwane
ke ntletsentletse
ho aparwa dimini skirt
ntata ke enwa
hosasa ke yaane

RIBBON HANDS (TRANSLATION)

Ribbon hands
mama's little darling
decorative hands.
the way she is lazy
a coward retreats
anger is written on the forehead
children are like orphans
while the mother is still living
she goes to work
shoes stepping high
nails always wet with cutex
her boss knows her as
Mrs so and so
today the marriage is over
she lodged at owners houses
roll on
sweet sixteens
are plenty

WORK SHIRE

Kana ka sega phefo
ka ralla dinaga
ka rakana le monna
are Yorkshire
England kwa moroba
tiro emo batla mabogo
ka e bona
ka e tshwantshanya
le small heaven
nare yona ke Yorkshire
tlogela botsoropa wena
bothakga gabo rekwe
banna ba kwa Tsetse Tsitsi
mesong ba sadisa dikobo
kwa Jo'burg
ba bolawa ke more kom

WORK SHIRE (TRANSLATION)

I ran away
skipping the border
and met a man
saying Yorkshire
England in luxury
job seekers
go for it
small heaven
identify yourself
with Yorkshire
stop laziness
money buy no neatness
men at Tsitsikama
say goodbye to blanket
in Jo'burg
they are told to come tomorrow

MR BROWN˟

Brown
white
behind my unit
I see you
today and everyday
painting
my unit
in weird colours
Mr Brown
drowning in my soup
playing hide and seek
with the spider man
you are his bread
for lunch
stop your
jumble sale
games
Mr Brown

˟Mr Brown is a cockroach

PUSH ASIDE SQUEAKY

Push aside squeaky
sky scrubbed
to the blue
door to door
volle homey hi 1
in chaff pozies
them no good never buy
mashakara is hulle mos 2
pounding hearts knock
search
suna papa nana 3
mochochonona drive 4
van corner
bafedile 5
binne kasie 6
in eight kant
cancer bantwana 7
drum ten distribute
bullet holes in their pockets
ba tsokotsa diketle 8
dikgogedi di kolobetsa matjhoba 9
goody goody boys
scaffolding
bunch to bunch
in cook dladlas 10
push aside sqeaky
pidi pidi 11
ha ena meno 12

1. going home in high spirits
2. they are a gang
3. kiss your father
4. streamline
5. they are finished
6. in the location
7. white city babes
8. they rinse kettles
9. attractive flowers drown sangoma's power sticks
10. shebeen
11. chirp of a cricket
12. doesn't have teeth

PART 5:

POEMS BY ALLAN KOLSKI HORWITZ:

CIRCLING BRUSSELS	51
WAVES IN A TUNNEL	51
VOICE	52
THE BRIDGE	53
SKY WHEEL	54
PAYING RESPECT	54
THOUSANDS OF YEARS	55
PEARL	55
SUBMARINE	56
HEAVENLY MUSIC	57
BARE DREAM	57
TRACE	58
WORKING THE LEVERS	59
YOUR HANDS WITH SILVER RINGS	59
THE BALLAD OF LEWIS AND ELS SLEEPING IN THE STREET SHOWS	60
FAITH IN THE WORLD	62
EMPTY BELLIES TREMBLE	62
WHO WILL MAKE THE MARKS	63

CIRCLING BRUSSELS

Smelling of grass near the hangars
a soldier lies with his rustless kit
in wait for predators
designated enemies

perhaps the grass moves with the wind
like the hum of his mother's heart
when his sinews were still
five curling fingers sculpting
a nipple

in the duty-free shops
men and women choose
what they can afford
boards flip destinations
planes circle Brussels

wombs contract without mercy

each child born
should have a pillow
flowing with milk

each child created
play in the windy grass
stroking the fingers
of that rampant mechanic

cramped he lies
near the hangars
automatic

WAVES IN A TUNNEL

In a garden on a swing
a woman stirs
tinkling her sides
a white gown laps
bronzed legs
a fat man stands quietly
inclined

they cannot see far
waves curl into a tunnel
sunset swathes the garden
amber gold and purple
the tang of salt suffuses flowers

he asks: lemon or milk?

her shoulders
a deep bell
as he turns
to his tray

VOICE

Confronted by
a Death Head that jeers
at broken skulls
that says:
I am free
to kill
even
as I love

when wires were cut
searchlights blacked
barracks razed
the bunks the grey blankets
striped inmate
pyjama-shrouds
scorched by flame
you looked up at last
to the sun
opened and stretched
you turned from the ashes

now we stand
looking into pits dug by prisoners
spades in our hands
guards scream
place them neatly in piles
to the side
of the burial-grounds
Death Head barks everywhere
tilts its bone-nose
as wind rises with day's earth
fragrance faint but
insistent

Human
you are free to fill graves
but you live also beyond
power-beast

we turn from the pits
you who has been there for so long
I remnant weaving on the edge
of that abyss
we stand back from the graves
turn to the guards
their faces narrow
as gun barrels
we open our hands to them

day is bright
the Death Head
spits
somehow the pits are covered
even as we sing
O mother
this song which sings itself
when the human heart
cannot bear its witness

THE BRIDGE

When all strength had left him
all songs departed
an old man took him and laid him
by a bridge on the National Road
convoys of sheep-farmers and water-diviners
kommandant in a Casspir
passed him there
and he lay past noon without stirring

it was a roving jackal that drove
him from under the bridge
to the lime-washed walls of a donga
there for the gathering
of sun-flower seeds

from the pondoks outside Christiana
out of the shade of a dry eucalyptus
an old woman fed him pap
and a trickle of tea
so at last under that blue sky
he felt strong in the knees

SKY WHEEL

Brushed cobalt sky
half-moon sails
in hooded silver
sky wheel swings
swallows flutter
moon rises clear
as wings slide and tear
the moisture
why am I so immobile
on my feet?
everything else
is flying
as far as I can see
everything else
is simply flying

PAYING RESPECT

A curl swept out of place
tendril dipping out of line
greyish cut across the face
unlike the dumb
flesh fines faces pay
recording dreams

another trace splits
the eyes from mouth
convulsion of both
north and south

> old woman crossing the street
> wind blows
> her hair cannot refuse

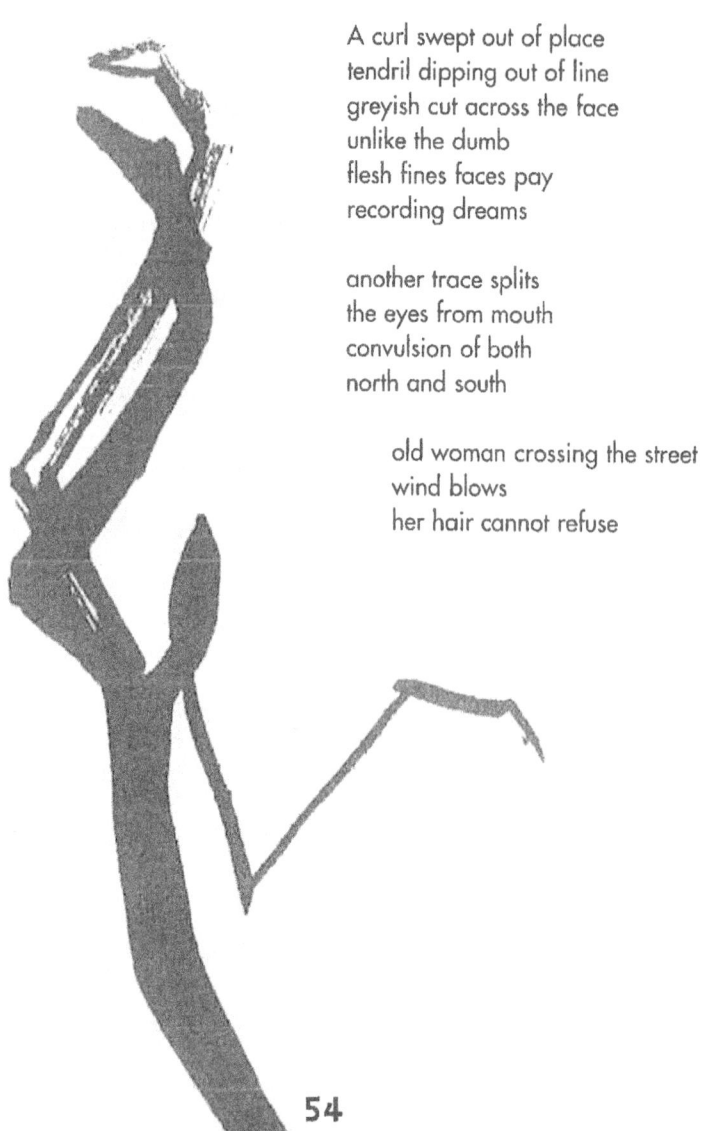

THOUSANDS OF YEARS

We laid him by the tomb
cut out of soft rock
and placed spices
in the shroud
to sweeten
the passage of worms

we wound the white robe tight
dug deeper
so he could envelop
the earth he loved
sanctify the body of his Father
we dug deep so he could lie alone
rolled a boulder
against the mouth
and wept for our Master
wailing men and women
rolling a boulder
the size of Sin

Now we say:
rise Master
rise from death
we have prayed out of need
for a miracle
we are tired of crisis

PEARL

I think of you lying
before the sun
by the ocean

beside you in the sand
a glowing lucid tranquil
pearl

and you string the pearl
between your breasts

I think of you as I work
with these words
turning them inside out
like a shirt
embroidered but useful

naked by the ocean
you stretch to put on
this poem

only a wispy covering
for your radiant breathing body
before the sun
strung on the sand
with that pale luminous
pearl

SUBMARINE

In this quiet flat between the coast of rocks
the Main Road with its pizza-ovens
supermarkets and hair-salons
I am a submarine
propellers idling
in the purple marks of memory
diamonded by shoals of star-fish
articulating all about my honed tower
my jutting cone
sonic stabbing

I lie feverish in bed
racked by virus

massacres at vigils
balaclaved mercenaries
in the pay of secret police
throughout walled suburbs
sirens advertise the brutish call
of armed response
I turn to other texts
accounts of ecstasy and hope
illumination and release
snow-leopards invisible
in the white fasts
of the Himalayan wilderness

beside me lies my hero-self
childhood companion
from whom I have not the courage
to lift away the winding sheet
I cannot now bare myself
brain too unsteady
the window ajar
who can tell which other presence
may slip in between day end
and day break?

with sudden force
I recall a lover
fond eyes and slashed wrists
shocked by my support
for the Red Brigades
my dangling in the cashless vault
of Art
she worked for international banks
exchanging her palette
for a screen of zeroes

now snared by this unpeeling
I wonder how my bed
can be positioned
to receive the sun

submarine at ever deeper depths
idling under dreamy weeds
scintillating
though the depth
is black and blue and blotting
star-fish spreading
till I cannot pin
their points of light

HEAVENLY MUSIC

Thick sweet smell
of white bellflowers
a narcotic to bring easy death
dagga fumes hanging
from a pondok's ceiling
on metal walls
a broken mirror
torn calendar
October in Zululand
February along the Kei
they sit on boxes
hush of evening
too bruised to offer
more than a murmur

perfumes from the trading place
explode against the yellow lights
of armoured cars
bellflowers
droop into evening
alien in the highveld chill
round Diagonal Street
lines of workers at taxi-ranks
defy the flesh that's nightly burnt

then from their places
they switch on the highway's rhythm
purr of engines along
the barrel of curves
switch on
jackhammers thundering
underground
they lean forward
to hear the heavenly music

BARE DREAM

Trekking through mountains
thorny flowers and boulders
cut by rivers and fences
raw security blades
his hand locked in hers
faces pressed to the mesh
they passed farmhouses
sheds full of meat
they climbed fluttering
from buckling wire
beating against it like moths
then tipping over
they breached the no-go zone
to reach the city
low round buildings in clay
a city of the sea
and heavy industry
they returned to their home
but all was changed
three bare rooms
empty of artifice
of idols
she cracked twigs for a fire
readied the cooking pots
he lay on a mat
figuring a dark unspeaking body
but once she appeared
with a steaming plate
in an old dress
scented with his first kisses
he flamed as never before

in the morning when
children from the garden
threw open the shutters
he stood naked on the window sill
and stared at them calmly

TRACE

Do you remember the nights
the child
called you to the window
to watch lightning streak
above the jacaranda trees?

trace the ages
mother's milk thick with salt
gruel blood cordite chocolate
cinnamon of baked pears
father's lined face after work
tense and introspective

watch a film:
men and women
meet and flirt
sense the soul-dynamo
charging their
destiny
lifting
the ball they must throw up
and catch

WORKING THE LEVERS

Agitprop
they say (that is the intellectual
middle-class
with its buttered
arse)
get rid of
slogans
those miserably poor
expressions

give us
rich text
acrobatics
in Form
banquets of
succulent philosophies

even our
rutted experience
more savoured than their
struggle
to survive
the lack
of light

the Individualistic
Middle-class
Professional
cultivated
not entirely heartless

YOUR HANDS WITH SILVER RINGS

Your hands with the silver rings
I will slide onto your fingers
with which to join the wings
of all beginnings

your hands full with instants
wrung from sorrow
your fingers sleek with silver
with which to solder

your fingers full with instants
wrought from gauzy motion
the white the yellow the black
butterflies of the garden

blue becomes purple
silver rings all whorled
with sweetness become
the wings of our beginning

THE BALLAD OF LEWIS AND ELS

Ja, check those waves
This night
These swells running
From the Island
To the Point
Though stars are bright but cold
Hearts are hot and bold
But first check the moon
The round pale moon
Here at the southern tip
A stone's throw
From where the ice-bergs dip
Ups and downs
Bass and treble notes
An interrupted dream
In which a sigh and a scream
Float
King Lewis the Dealer
Has a head
Full of worries
And Els
She's had her fill
Of Lewis' sorries
Lekker lekker night
Sweet with dagga
And brandy's delight
Rollers crash like the first
Big Bang
The moon's blank
A hand moves with a knife
No stone ever sank
Without causing strife
Lewis' got his brain in fever
As for Els
What can possibly relieve her?
This lingering night
Full of blush
And the dice's bright eye
But who's the one to knock the blocks?
Who's the one to shit hot rocks?
Who's the one with mirror shades?
And who's the one walking slowly
Over their graves?
Ja, Lewis
They take you from behind
They do their job

A rival gang from Windermere
They pin you down
And shred your spear
Only Twenty-eight
But there's no denying
Fate
When you was a kid
You had it made
The manne said
Watch your balls
Lewis is ready and steady
So sterk the devil's afraid
But tonight the twist is turned
King of White Pipes
Gets his fingers burned
Els has him by the hand
A casual stroll without precaution
They're talking of this and that
His affairs her last abortion
They're catching a breeze
On a shell-filled beach
Lewis sucks the juice from his peach
Ag, lovers are blind
Rivals
They nail him
Lewis drops to the sand
They jab him like bees
They take his bag
And his bunch of keys
Els quakes on the edge of their razors
But the 'Lover Boys' panic
They take off quick
She's left untouched
Though her heart is sick
Down by the sea
Waves wash
Grey gulls soar
Els sobs
While Lewis lies gored
On the Flats
On the Mountain
On the wind-blown Vlei
Blood on the children
Of the Khoi the Dutch
The Xhosa and the Javanese
Blood on the pine

The protea
Port Jackson brought from overseas
It's almost dawn
Will he live or will he die?
Her heart breaks
As she hears him sigh
"Hey Baby
What you been doing?
My body aches
Everything's gone hazy"
The moon withholds her light
Lewis shivers
Els bends as he clutches
Her tight
And the Flats
And the Mountain
And the blue-green Bay
But it's she who screams
Falls to her side
Poor Els
She writhes now
On the rising tide
She stood by Lewis
Ready to raise
An heir to his crown
Ja, Els was carrying his jewel
But he's cut her down
Her mouth foams with bloody drool
His gangster's blade has put a stop
To all her rigmaroles
Her doubts her fears
Her night patrols
Carrying his special bag
With all those pills
That mind-blowing smoke
Lewis's fortune was no joke
A manic thrust
Fatal surprise
Now she's dead on the rocks
While he's bathed
In ghostly beams
In her womb forever still
The child formed from their
Passion's will
Lewis couldn't stand to leave her
So it seems
Or did he hear
double-cross in her screams?
He strokes her hand

He's whispering
"I need you
Come with me, lovey
It's Lewis
Let me lick the red
From your lips"
Watch him wipe
A tear as it drips
On the Flats
On the Mountain
On the Bay
No one stirs though it's break
Of day
Phantom lovers
Still by the sea
The moon strolls faint
Spray shoots to the sky
The south-easter rolls
Waves run high
Down by the southern tip
Bright stars fade
On the cold handle
Of the bloody blade
Mannenberg's candle
In Love's parade

SLEEPING IN THE STREET
SHOWS FAITH IN THE WORLD

Put your back down
on the pavement

lie down and be vulnerable:
we are broken people

those who have stripped
everything

sleep in the street - footsteps and the beat:
a lamb, accepting

on the street at night when lamplight
is dim:

arm arched on concrete
under the full glare and chill

the burning scorch of stars and neon
and hurrying

> To sleep and dream
> is to climb a ladder
>
> only the destitute
> or the feeble of mind
>
> or
> youth believe in
>
> on the highway of the world
> with boldness

EMPTY BELLIES TREMBLE

Bellies tremble and
with hungering fingers
take out knives (such hope
-lessness) waiting for night
for cloud for quiet and sleeping sentries
we wait to fill ourselves
a little

may the night of growling dogs
ignore our pad
this night which covers
sentries whose cocked
revolvers wake to jam us
at the windows

we walk
filling shack-towns
new planets
with our loot our staples
our dream-machines
we shack-dwellers of the end-zones
we take the last bus
to zones of plenty of green
of sharp fangs

passing trees and flower-beds
freezers stocked
with meat and vegetables
passing the walls
of these mansions of the wise
and worthy who still howl
though enclosed with
healthy children
passing all these things
we who have
next to nothing
except
the throttled air
of hungering
we take out our knives

WHO WILL MAKE THE MARKS

Reality
of motion and trance

world is

elands leaping into the moon

dust covers the table
dust covers the face of the man
at the table
dust covers the face of the man
at the table and dust covers his pen

dust covers and who

will lift a hand to wipe the man and the table
who will dust his pen

who will make marks
in the dust

PART 6:

PERFORMANCE POEMS BY IKE MBONENI MUILA

RISHILE	65
KHUMBANI	65
MY BETTER HALF	66
BLOOMER JO'BURG	66
MUYAHAVHO	67
MADICE	68
SAMBA NDOU	69
SECRETARY BIRD	70
NEVADA JOE	70
ELELWANI N.P. MUILA	71
LOVE INDEX	72
VAN SIDLANGOZWANE	72
DONGOLOLO LA TSIMBI	73
WASEKHAYA	74
SMART ALECS	75
MUENDANYI	76
FOR THE WOMAN I LOVE	77
MAVHELE A VHATHU	78

RISHILE [1]

Open sky
shame in disgrace
who worship
father be
that name
madly frustrated
in favour
of bloodshed come
that will never be
as it is not
in any
heaven come
pity strip
their names
in tartarus torn
tattered naked
forgive us
our emotions
carelessly driven
against us
in shambles
practice
against us
high and low
on a daily
bloodshed come
corruption
given this day
our daily bread
forever
in their
kingdom
bloodshed come
fallen be
their glory
bloodshed come
forever
and ever
shame
overcome
bottomless pity
bums come
eternal kiss
the devil come
disengage a muddy
bloody well
low and no more

KHUMBANI [2]

In a snail
kumbani [3]
khumbani
small one
ndingavela [4]
golden lay
soul finger pressure
malkop caravan
lang one seun
jakarumba [5]
four five
base two
staffrider
ngolovane [6]
hill extension
gaat sak
pilikie vonkel
toe sluit
wat lag jy
Jan van Riebeeck
dink jy
gaat sak
ek is ou
father chrismas
buck short botsotso
skop en skiet
Jan pampoene
spare twine
mbazo slash [7]
Soweto
buck short garage
grand covered
workshop
rema jy nou [8]
gaat sak
bless kop
masana [9]
hoe lyk jy
nou dae
spanner kop
bra kate skaap [10]

1. sunrise
2. in a snail
3. collect
4. peep
5. foot
6. carriage
7. axe
8. refuse
9. sun beams
10. friendship

MY BETTER HALF
FOR ISABELLA 17/08/93

Love nest well
in hard times
bad times
together
in difficulties
cooldrinks
both of us
down the bottom
of hardship
hard times
mafanya life
money here
money there
in good times
buy a cooldrink
Jo'burg our home
our stable
window pane
drink it cool
my better half
we build a home
on top of a rock
our Jo'burg home
we had hard times
in difficulties together
come rain come
though thunder storms
my better half
thou shalt never
wither

1. Stay Jo'burg
2. stay old man
3. a better off person
4. around town
5. I spin around town
6. these days
7. look this way
8. peep secretly
9. while away time
10. for sleep
11. for rising up

BLOOMER JO'BURG [1]

Bloomer
Bloomer madala [2]
ek is 'n ou
Texan Terries [3]
binne in die toene [4]
change deurdlana
op en af
bloomer madala
bloomer
bloomer madala
ek spin
in die toene [5]
ek nou die dag [6]
jy sal never nie
skarf kry nie
check lapha site [7]
calaza madala site [8]
ek vang hulle
is net dresh
die een
is 'n ou mudryseni [9]
die ander een
is 'n ou malala [10]
die laaste een
is 'n ou mavuka [11]
jy moet onthou
skyf is 'n proces
whereby
cigarette passes
from the owner
to the parasite
bloomer
bloomer madala

MUYAHAVHO

Muyahavho don't cry
please don't cry
kale kale [1]
ri tshe vhatuku [2]
gone are the days
we were young
vha tshi ri [3]
ndi gukulume [4]
illness tolerance
ri tshi la [5]
muno na madi [6]
water and salt
Muyahavho don't cry
please don't cry
half a loaf
of bread
for you to eat
without tea
to drink
take it cool
as it is
much better
please don't cry
early in the morning
you walk
to school
no money for lunch
a little smile
you reserve
release depression
promote a sense
of awareness
don't cry
please don't cry
your teacher
in the classroom
questions
loud and loud
in your head
for the missing
answer
you and me
forget not
the resort
to end the beginning
of our separate world
don't panic
please don't cry
one hungry afternoon
you walk
into the kitchen
you opening doors
of the kitchen unit
the pots are empty
no crumbs inside
everything
is speak and span
nothing
is left for you
don't cry
please don't cry
every dark cloud
has a silver lining
just stomach the pain
as if nothing
worries you
ungakhali akusizi [7]
work all covered
your way out
don't cry
please don't cry

1. long ago
2. when we were young
3. when they say
4. economising
5. when we eat
6. water and salt
7. don't cry, it's of no use

MADICE 1

Madice rework
double dwesh 2
two two
chances
over quiet storms
three one
second
one one
school wyd 3
person to person
chaff kop 4
amehlo ekati 5
bars two seven
knocks man
eight ou niks
one love service
school bar
six three
four five
six no nine
qualify dresh 6
coward double up
slaat uno 7
one time
double slash
lababa 8
senzeni 9
kha ndi sekene 10
Mutshinyani 11
kha u lile 12
ludzula back door 13
ndi maduvha mana 14
la vhutanu ndi mutshinyalo 15
davhani mifhululu 16
kha u lile 17
Dovhani 18
kha u lile 19
Vho Nyalitshalini 20
Ha Madala 21
Khakhu ngalife 22
Venda ni si luvhe 23
nga mufhetano 24
vhusiku sala nduni 25
mbuyavhuhadzi 26
yo vhuyela 27
zwi la zwa madekwe 28

Vho Muyanalo 29
khotsi a salani 30
king corn
manzhanzha 31
muthombo mmela 32
baphati la baphanya 33
ni vhalumelise 34
mutendeleki 35
Madilonga 36
thunda nnda 37
Mudangawe 38
blesskop 39
masana 40
ya vhonala 41
curved mirror
hunchback
showground
mutsho usa tshi 42
tano la talelani 43
kha la sun valley 44
no dice
sikabopha 45
masia gwala 46
kha la Venda 47
dzenengu 48
li nyela nduni 49
mobile
tshiyamudane 50
thevhele ya matshimba 51
Rambwana 52
Tshamato 53
lo huvha kholomo 54
nguluvhe ya milo 55
tshitumbani 56
u nala gaku 57
ndi u vhumbuluwa 58
kha mufumbu 59
mazishe 60
Codesa nonstop
laat hulle brand
anti clockwise
laat hulle verby
clockwise
man
to the left
last banduza 61
smaak lekker
like a chicken
in the oven

first beshu 62
spoja wakker 63
teka u famba 64
nyangalambuya 65
bring back
latter days
how mean jy
nou vole
symbolic these days
mbo 66
mmi ndi mmi 67
mma ndi mma 68
first floor
smokers corner
plamkfontein
plate
pondokkie
zoll no fuss
boroko shampi 69
rough jive
mapunapuna 70
ace base
high
madresh 71
dance
blah for me
ngadealer 72
ndangala spy 73
roller
pavement
night
madala site 74
dosalie 75

1. dice
2. two
3. open up
4. hide
5. cats eyes
6. three
7. one
8. slap
9. what have we done
10. let me be serious
11. name of a person
12. ululate
13. pleasure
14. four days
15. on the fifth day is crisis
16. ululate workers
17. ululate
18. name of a person
19. ululate of a person
21. name of a place
22. name of a place, meaning, 'when it's sunrise'. Let it perish.
23. don't worship
24. with pestering
25. to rise up early - Venda proverb
26. a divorcee
27. is back fo
28. evening matters
29. name of a person
30. Venda proverb, meaning,' Fathers who angrily left their family'
31. sorghum
32. sorghum cob
33. barbarian
34. do pass my greetings
35. a wanderer
36. name of a person
37. hunch back in the open
38. name
39. bald
40. sun beams
41. it appeared
42. non stop
43. show off
44. at sun valley
45. cut and bind
46. off track
47. at Venda
48. hooligan
49. excrete in the house
50. toilet
51. heap of shit
52. name of a dog, meaning, 'small bowl'
53. name of a dog
54. howling at a cow
55. a pig who eats too much - a Venda proverb for a glutton
56. pig sty
57. hunger strike
58. roll over
59. left over remnants of grain
60. let's smoke
61. zoll stub
62. first to have a turn
63. zoll stub
64. take and go
65. Venda word for godess of wealth
66. here you are
67. giving is giving
68. mothers are mothers
69. empty slip
70. naked
71. lady; a Jamaican word
72. opportunist
73. baboon
74. sacredly
75. nothing

SAMBA NDOU

Elephants bath
samba ndou 1
vho shavhela ngeno 2
mushumo khwatha 3
dzhavhelo bandani 4
vhashumi 5
mushumo 6
u shavha zwanda 7
butter shoes on
foot prints
caterpillar
eligible
ebile 8
dia signer 9
ebile 10
dia stamper 11
shwelebaba 12
shelenkosiyami 13
let the drums
echo roll
bongo man
silver
sunshine
duluni 14
vigroece current 15
salvation spy
papier sak
from Naledi
to Jeppe
fishline
join the press
sardines bite
Saldanha bay
love affairs
jikeleza train 16
vole
bashemane 17
ba bapala 18
sigangeni 19
canada dry
music injection

1. elephants bath
2. they came up running
3. work grow stronger
4. fortress in the belt
5. workers
6. work
7. is afraid of hands
8. more over
9. they sign
10. more over
11. they stamp
12. please father
13. please my Lord
14. storage
15. Latin-Afro-English meaning, 'to eat'
16. round about
17. the boys
18. playing
19. in the field

SECRETARY BIRD

time spread
credit
teachers court
coward ghost
viro lock
broken lock
cook dladla slot 1
dimmer
fumbling repair
piles up
andrew jeans
a genius
ice lid
stove pipe
rock
too tight
a nut
too can crack
dimmer
brokers pan
dish
a lonely long
logger dancer
dimmer
skelm key
hard liner
rubber neck
dimmer
in great times
buy your time
enjoy the fun
before the sun
enjoys you
dimmer
special kite
cement
cellular figure
celebrity
dimmer

secretary bird
covered jersey
mobile and available
emapozie 2
dimmer
skipper bar
block buster
score
dimmer bella stones
dimmer bushy
dimmer wasekhaya 3

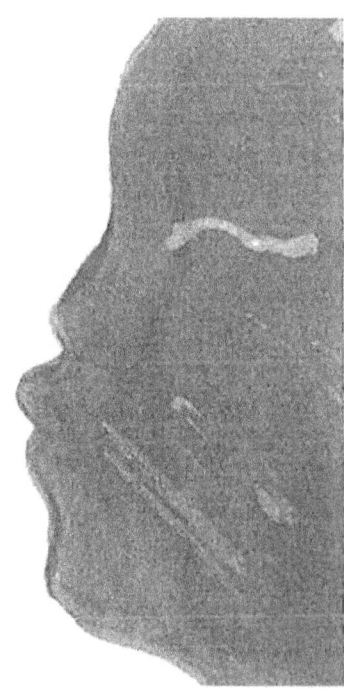

1. dladla: home
2. slot
3. home buddy
4. drink
5. better
6. let us pull
7. together at one
8. tyres
9. better

NEVADA JOE

Nevada Joe
take no hours
on end
habula jaws 3
habula buddy
happiness
if I were
to buy you
flowers
what colour
would you prefer
habula jaws
now that love
is colourless
survey nou
half moja joe 5
I am not here
to play you
an hour man flint
masidonse 6
kanyekanye 7
habula jaws
gibberish
one love
one stand
under
one umbrella
binder masonda 8
across
the white line
survey moja 9
happiness now

ELELWANI N.P. MUILA 10/94

ranga u thetshelesa
iwe mafuka duvha
vha muvhuya
phedza dza nga
tshikwatamba
tsha luranga
ponze ifa
yo nambatela
mulivho
la u tavhela
u li ore
muoki wa lo
phalalani
tsengela tsiwana
fhasi dzi thavhani
vhu ima
mbidi na khongoni
Muila matavhelo
buka
li sa ori duvha
muthannga musekene
mutamba na vhokunaho
muthannga
a sa li vhutete
nga u shavha
u tetemela
wa thumbu
i no pangwa
mutavha ya xa
Muila thende
ya lufheto
Muila tshivhindi
tsha nguluvhe
a sa li phinimini

IN MEMORY OF N.P. MUILA 10/94 (TRANSLATION)

*listen you
who wears
the sun
collectors
of my head
of cattle
a pumpkin stem
dies attached
to a coconut
make hay
while the sun shines
in any case
worship not
by pestering
assist
the orphan's protector
down the mountains
down the station
of impala and zebras
for an animal
who never basks
in the sun
a slender gentleman
who washes
amongst the pure
for shivering from fear
a gentleman who does not
eat soft porridge
with a stomach
which when
filled with sand
becomes flat
daybreak is sacred
the handle
of a stirring spoon
to him is sacred
forbidden a white liver
he who does not eat
red beak honey birds*

LOVE INDEX

love index
of discomfort
eloff street
candy collar
maravela 1
corner
market and nugget
cake ndaba 2
pitika 3
washing brake
coffee bar
gauteng maboneng 4
commisioner
benrose
ellispark
calibres
tapela 5
tapepe spy 6
kom kry
skhumba touch 7
salvation spy
dry skin
stop station
service touch line
slander
waterproof
dramatic
order disorder
in diguise
wardrobe
blinkers
munching
exclusive
blue mass

VAN SIDLANGOZWANE 8 07/95

Stealing
van sidlangozwane
skuwet under
cosset
nou skiloog
ou koeke moer
se sister
smoke down
mzamo 9
drum ten
cook tycoon
moleko 10
dink jy
phambili 11
volle iets
wonderlik
of kanjani 12
pump jy
nou proper vol
ou koeke moer
se sister
shanty
dae diesel
engine
gum gum
guys
bubbling gums
wat gat aan
service station
draadlosie maker
pump jy mos
nou natural oulik
of kanjani

1. rebels
2. news
3. overturn
4. in the lights
5. pull
6. stealing
7. skin
8. stealing
9. effort
10. temptation
11. forward
12. how

DONGOLOLO LA TSIMBI

Dongololo la tsimbi
ba rekisa
malana le mohodu
madombolo
le magwinya
dongololo la tsimbi
ndi la vhurwa
dongololo la tsimbi
li bva vhurwa
a locomotion ready
to swallow afresh
an early
dressed up platform
to their destination
basopa
platform one
kusuka
amaphepha
kusala
amakhadibox
an iron snake
vomits people
in large numbers
to their destination
ba rekisa
malana le mohodu
modombolo
le magwinga
dongololo la tsimbi
ndi la vhurwa
dongololo la tsimbi
li bva vhurwa

AN IRON CENTIPEDE (TRANSLATION)

*An iron centipede
they are selling
intestinal meat
dumplings
and fat cakes
an iron centipede
of the south
an iron centipede
is from the south
a locomotion ready
to swallow afresh
an early
dressed up platform
to their destination
watch out
platform one
out flies papers
cardboard boxes
remains behind
an iron snake
vomits people
in large numbers
to their destination
they are selling
intestinal meat
dumplings
and fat cakes
an iron centipede
of the south
an iron centipede
is from the south*

WASEKHAYA 1

Moenie worry nie
wasekhaya
luister baba
Patlene
my bra Kate
moenie worry nie
wasekhaya
Mudau wa Thenzheni la
malowa ndila 2
isikhathi 3
siyashwabana 4
wasekhaya
ek kom nou
langs aan
besoek
my ma se kind
ngisaphumakanje 5
wasekhaya
ndi matombonyane 6
ek onthou
dae brakate 7
oorla ou Jacky
ou Mujackwana 8
van alle trade
witty hy van
nou die dag clevers
clevers
hulle chisela 9
nine nine 10
binnekant
in danyane 11
seven jares
in danyane
is maar net
soos peanuts
clevers gaan hulle
nine nine
vir jares baba
hierso slaat jy
katarie mzala 11
kom kry
ons drink mbomboza 12
rook tarries
van die one one
muntwana is galore 13
speel jy

ou maqumbane 14
soft music ook
jy kom kry
amapapa 15
before
gidlary time 16
gatas kry jou 17
waarlike nog
vir haba 18
wasekhaya
hulle vat jou
vir zwothe zwothe 19
bakhiwa 20
daasy in
badcompany
in vir jares
kom kry
jy is nou
binnekant
vir cheap stuff
kak stories
jy kom kry
uyabonakala baba 21
eshashalazini 22
binnekant danyane
van daarso
jy dosalie kry
my bra Kate
net gidlary
soos 'n three star
banana oukapie
emakhayeni 23
jy is ou
bra Mugeorgerna
in danyane
jy gaan ou
Georginah wees
of Polinah
bantwana 24
waarso
ou Tiekie boy
waarso
ou Bambo
en ou Libumba
wakker wees
mahlalaeshushu 25
vuka umaulele 26
geen njalaza 27
for worries

1. home buddy
2. Venda praise name for Madau clan and also a proverb
3. time
4. expires
5. I am on my way
6. very scarse
7. friend or a brother
8. name of a person
9. hard labour
10. 'openly' or, 'fair and square'
11. jail
12. guitar cousin
13. liquer
14. babe
15. babe
16. food
17. sleep
18. police
19. for nothing
20. all assorted
21. fellow person
22. you show up or come over
23. in the open
24. at home
25. babes
26. drunkard
27. wake up from sleep
28. time

SMART ALECS

Smart alecs
isicamtho my sister 1
luister nou mojanero 2
jump tyd 3
mmatimba 4
van gister
maubani 5
izolo 6
ek het jou
gawietie 7
om te se
alles verstaan
sweet no mukatakata 8
nee
jy is half moja 9
bo dae gebou
alles is covered
en los chandies 10
finya-skuks 11
ek raak
vole vole
tot daarby die
dollie my ousie
skuwet nee 12
you sing me
a song
worth singing
smart alecs
is it good enough
that I sing?
wee sis Lizah
Mtaka Maduna 13
ngizokuthengela 14
ubhanana 15
nginama 16
pillowcase
nginama 17
shidi 18
nombhede 19
wokulala 20

1. can I talk to you
2. double meaning: "listen well" and "good enough"
3. after hours
4. in the evening
5. yesterday
6. yesterday
7. I told you
8. problems or troubles
9. better off
10. no hard feelings
11. glorifying a person
12. "sharp", "okay" or "covered"
13. Maduna's daughter
14. I will buy you
15. banana
16. I have
17. I have
18. sheet or bedspread
19. and a bed
20. to sleep in

MUENDANYI

our home
is an attraction
of sorry sight
roof over shacks
tin house
in the area
of sinkholes
vha phalali
vha da
na vhulombo
dzo no siela
matumba mbevha
do not
let them
fool you
with sugar
coated words
quick bucks
fancy cars
with angel-like
beautiful women
darkness shine
full of empty
promises
of heaven
on earth
wa la nawa
na vhanzhi
u zwimbela
dzi a talula
do not wait
at a distance
quite too
far remote
until it is
too late
madi a tevhuwa
ukumbela
ndi vhudenga

home a frightful
plight
trust me
you will learn
to teach
how one should
understand
a bridge
of sorrow
in a privilege
dispute

MUENDANYI *
(TRANSLATION)

our home
is an attraction
of sorry sight
roof over shacks
tin house
in the area
of sinkholes
people rescue
come over
poverty stricken
having left behind
a home for rats
do not
let them
fool you
with sugar
coated words
quick bucks
fancy cars
with angel-like
beautiful women
darkness shine
full of empty
promises
of heaven
on earth
if you eat beans
with many people

constipation
strikes individuals
do not wait
at a distance
quite too
far remote
until it is
too late
spilt water
cannot be
collected
home a frightful
plight
trust me
you will learn
to teach
how one should
understand
a bridge
of sorrow
in a privilege
dispute

* persons name also meaning to protect or bring together.

FOR THE WOMAN I LOVE

exclusive
black and white
arrogant
blue collar
two piece
of farcical
school dungarees
frisky exercise
ri tanganya
madanda a pfene
venda la vha
la ha maladze
mapfene a tsitsa
vhana
one after
the other
over and over
again
again and again
laughter after laughter
over and over
emangwaneni
frisky time
you take away
my scribbling pads

FOR THE WOMAN I LOVE (TRANSLATION)

*exclusive
black and white
arrogant
blue collar
two piece
of farcical
school dungarees
frisky exercise
we bind
a baboon's hands
Venda remains
a peaceful place
baboons put down
their children* 1
*one after
the other
over and over
again
again and again
laughter after laughter
over and over
"a pleasure home"* 2
*frisky time
you take away
my scribbling pads*

1. Venda proverb about peace and happiness
2. an old lady told me about this place near Bergville which is a place of happiness. Also a nickname for a disco in Rockville

MAVHELE A VHATHU [1]

Father now that
you are home
the question
of who deserves
the crust
or crumbs
leaves much
to be desired

for no reason
nga Mutshekwa [2]
to uncle Shangoni boy

for no reason
nga Mutshekwa
to my mother
kitchen girl

for no reason
nga Mutshekwa
to my grandmother
girl friday

for no reason
      mavhele a vhathu
for no reason
      o liwa nga mini [3]
for no reason
      o liwa nga pfene [4]
for no reason
      pfene ndi nnyi [5]
for no reason
      pfene ndi nne [6]
melting pot of love
bring people to light
who hurt others
for their next meal
and for pleasures
muri u vhavhaho
u bva tsindeni [7]

1. people's maize
2. Venda exclamation of surprise
3. what ate the maize
4. baboon ate the maize
5. who is a baboon
6. I am a baboon
7. a Venda proverb: "a bitter tree starts at it's roots"

PART 7:

POEMS BY ANNA VARNEY

ON THE 1ST DAY HE SAT UNDER THE MANGO TREE	80
QUESTIONS AND UNBURNT ANSWERS	80
I ALWAYS THINK I KNOW YOU	81
PLUNGING	82
WE IS ALL FRACTURED	82
MOVEMENTS	82
SHE DRINKS	83
THE SHITMASTERS	83
STARTING WITH CIRCUMCISION	84
AFTER THE RESCUE FROM SLAVERY	85
PAGES AMONG OTHERS	86
BELOVED COUNTRY CRYING	86
SPLIT	87
CONGENIALITY	88
THE COMING TOGETHER	88
WE EAT OUT PLANET	89
SHADOW	89
DANCE	89
SIGH	89
1. AUTUMN / 2. ELECTIONS	90
REFLECTION	91

ON THE 1ST DAY HE SAT UNDER A MANGO TREE . . .

shadows cast
without a rustle
reflections
are not the thing
itself
days slide
silently by
against the rising
and the falling
over sheer
water
dipping insects
staccato
the ripples
silver and turquoise

        while cars race
        and a hand plunges
        into a child's face

one step
may well be all
one should ever take
in a life span

QUESTIONS AND UNBURNT ANSWERS

I am
but I am in the wind

we turn rage into
sweet puddings
serve it up
in large portions
(they call what they're doing
    reconstruction
 their reconstruction
 knows
 nothing about foundations)

we know change
means war
we move
slowly   slowly
as a sigh
reaching for hands of our children
as we cross the roads

I ALWAYS THINK I KNOW YOU

I always think I know you
until I hear you speak
I always believe we are family
until you show me
the chasm between us
could kill us

I reach for your warm hand
and find it filled with ammunition
I reach for your warm hand
and find it amputated

I reach for you
and strike
because what I find
is so strange
causes such loneliness

PLUNGING

she leans against a paper boat
her black dress
floating along the roadside

a sickle moon reflects
in umber water
then she wakes - k n o w i n g -
she must n e v e r dip her cold hands
into heated basins

having tea on the balcony
later that morning she asks
the woman with the long nose
(which she knows she ought not to
watch) if she'd like nose in
her tea
    she spills grains of brown all over
the white
puts the sugar
lid into her coffee mug
    offers a presentation of scones with cerise
jam and billowing
cream
she says:
hug me
- planting kisses
all over
Noses' cheek
clicking her
nails

on her feet shoes
of raw
umber shine

WE IS ALL FRACTURED

i is fractured
you is fractured
we all need a strong medicine
a healing song

        the night is a dancer
        under pools of light
        everything is wet shiny
        skins

our poor heart jus' needs
a little rest
to breathe in deep
to release
a long whistle

then we'll move
to find the dancer
under layers
of our sorrowful activities

MOVEMENTS

a black spider ran across my hand
this morning
        [was contemplated in]
- a cliche   my mind
        [contaminated   ]

I churn out rotten stuff
the air has mummified
hands may've had purpose
- forgotten now we bungle
doing our inadequacies
    2 foreigners arrive
    they bring in freshness
    from the outside
if we could be 1/2 as sharp
as the blows we receive
- someone's sharp

SHE DRINKS

she had nothing
so she drank
all her money
she has nothing
so she drinks
she is lost
but first
she lost everything
then she drank
now she drinks
she can't get work
that's why she's drunk
she's so drunk
she won't get work
she drinks
she drinks
because why
she's drunk

THE SHITMASTERS

Inside
I hear their footsteps
the plumbers place
their box of tools

Outside
plants hang against the sky
deep green
moist
looping threads
of coloured embroidery
Neighbouring yards
small lawns
in a row
The toilet flushes

In the world
            there is trouble
We sink under mounds
of death
though the decrepit
is left alive
between our walls

    The plumbers rinse the drain in acid
  They pull the chain

I once had a friend
who celebrated life
and loved
I believed in him
now I search
for what he knew

In this shadow world
light spilling onto plants
hints of joy
cycles of night and day
bear beckoning secrets
but I have no understanding

The house is quiet now
no more trouble here
no more shit

STARTING WITH CIRCUMCISION

Why do they call it 'circumcision'?
cutting away a piece of boys' skin
removing part of a girl's genitals
as though it's the same thing

Last night I went
for a walk
not too far
because rape
mugging

I found a tree
I could sit under
- to watch the sky
where no one could watch me
There was a smell of wet
ashes from the day
but no body was sleeping
there (though boughs sure looked
like limbs under the broken
moon)
Then I walked again
till I was no longer
running

Women please their men
- so they won't wander
Please the wanderers too
who 'won't leave Their Women'
for them (they've been too pleasing)
Women betray women oh
my fearful foolish Sisters

When they make love
to us they breathe: 'my sweet'
'feel my cock in your pussy'
We really think
it's only for us
Men
take on so much
responsibility
Take so much

Sometimes when we don't
understand
we are silent
Let the thing pass
Other times black and yellow blood
flows from the contest
Primal powers
*suffer injury**
When a river swims
we should not damn it

I turn the pages of my days
savagely
- tomorrow - tomorrow - tomorrow -

* Reference from the I Ching/Book of Changes -
The Receptive hexagram

AFTER THE RESCUE FROM SLAVERY

The people walk dumb
under the Eye
of the Master
who is so cruel

The people accept their fate
and no one speaks
about that

The people
never look into the face
of the Master
They carry their burdens
And no one speaks
about that

The people are angry
because someone has said something
about the Master
She said:
'He does not have to be our Master'

The people wait
The Master says:
'Stone her!'

The people always obey
their Master

PAGES AMONG OTHERS

- Madeleine's lover -
it does seem sometimes
he whittles at her
lacerates scars
with precision
- she so cross eyed -
sinister allusions
blur with apparition
she sits outside the back door
naked
teeth in her knuckles
- it is her hopefulness
that brings these troubles on
- leaning on
dreams must give way

    what is that there?
  - as all this grows smaller -
      it is the last
     of the strands
    on which to stand

also   sliding
     sliding

sometimes she tumbles
and drops
as if only in losing
can she expand
if she let go -
what would go on?

he walks in to joke / no jagged stuff
they laugh
the page turns

she reads

BELOVED COUNTRY CRYING

    a   girl   runs
    through   a   field   of   flowers
    her   hair   scented
    light   in   her   eyes

buildings explode
'terrorists' lash back
two marches take place
in parallel streets
one   about the Masses
one   about the Threat

drunkards
soaked senseless
cut their throats
or go on holiday
only to find an island
surrounded by a sea
of International Shit

the Sun is blacked out
and the Cause
nowhere to be found
Darkness
is it's Guardian

     NEWS FLASH
    a girl was shot in a field
    by snipers

SPLIT

Purple spread
against violet grey
still early night
twin lights shine
straight into my eyes

        jacaranda tree
        an oncoming car

I'm with one who loves me
that makes me happy
- but my lover has gone away
I don't know why -
I'm so filled with conflict and confusion
that's what's making me cry

    "my woman
    here is my phallus
    erect and hard
    beyond any comparison
    I am driven
    receive me"

    "my man here
    is my receptacle
    moist soft and warm
    beyond any comparison
    I am yearning
    enter me"

CONGENIALITY

You are the one
who did (or may still)
perform
glorious deeds
You are the one
who did (or may still)
heal
the most obscenely diseased
You are the one
who did (or may still)
force
a bayonet
down the mouth
of a child
You are the one
who did (or may still)
seek to profit
from a war meaningless
to you

At times you say:
'I see'
At times you say:
'I did not know'
Don't impress on me
your need
for congeniality

THE COMING TOGETHER

1.
A black butterfly
circles my studio
I believe
we are having a relationship
A second enters
and I see
they are quite unaware of me

2.
This power
I sometimes find
between myself and another
some name it chemistry
yes, that may be so
but it may also be fate
or a secret force
that draws us that way

WE EAT OUR PLANET

"technology is development"
applaud the couple

at dinner the woman eats
and eats to feed her tits
her husband has little else on his mind
they say
"there is no part ostrich
we do not use"
gravy running down their chins

   (while we applaud
    the wonders of the world
    Nature is appalled)

a man lies
tumbled on the beach
beside him a waiting
wheelchair
will he leave
his Fair Lady behind?

smell of piss as I ascend the stairs
to order a waffle and cream
on the way home
passing an escort agency
I'm startled
by a stranger's adoring smile

SHADOW

Yellow and white stone
reflect the light
in that place
where you walk

My thoughts of you
are with you

The shadow which trails
from your feet
are those

DANCE

Pulsing sweaty sweet
hand moulds my moves
last night -
how we danced!

butterfly kisses
hot muscle
throb
liquidsliding
I want to lie with you

SIGH

He
strokes my thighs
makes me a sea
of all women
  this one man/boy

I'm his world-woman
he visits me
from the skies I've planted him in
  I've made him mortal

1. AUTUMN / 2. ELECTIONS
28/4/94

1.
This is the season
of falling

I love ochre!
Burnt sienna
Now
it means the dying
away

How is this possible?
The ochre, the dying -
air so full
heavy just
before frost sets in
But Autumn is perfumed!
Loaded
with sandalwood and spices

Flame trees blaze
    - that moment before
a fire ceases - it's spark is
brightest

2.
 Spring
 is the political season -
 N O W I S T H E T I M E
our-vote-is-our-voice-vote-your-choice-our-vote-is-our-voice-vote-yours-
i flick out my hand
to catch a music

alone
on my way home i
open my window hold my fist
high
over the flyway

everyone is

VIVA
today

REFLECTION

overhead the blue
makes no distinction

Hillbrow
        Randburg
                Alex
                      Sebokeng
                              Orange Farm
                                      Soweto
Tembisa
        Pretoria
                Kagiso
                      Yeoville
                            Krugersdorp
                                    Katlehong
companions rest
by the roadside
on cool gravel

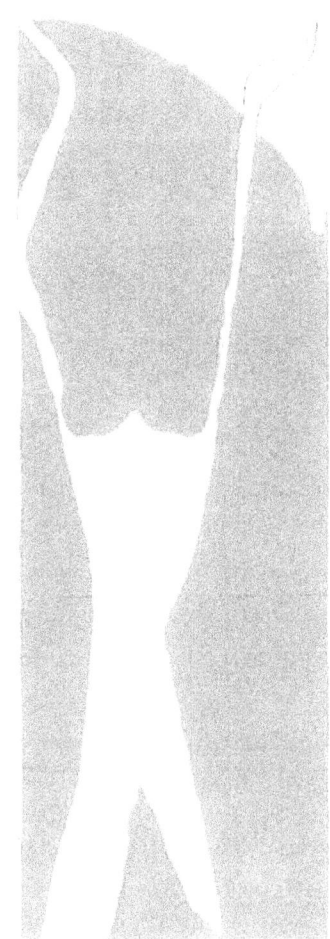

www.ingramcontent.com/pod-product-compliance
Lightning Source LLC
Chambersburg PA
CBHW080910230426
43666CB00014B/2663